Crime at Mayerling
The Life and Death of Mary Vetsera

Studies in Austrian Literature, Culture, and Thought

Translation Series

Georg Markus

Crime at Mayerling
The Life and Death of Mary Vetsera

With New Expert Opinions Following the Desecration of Her Grave

**Translated by
Carvel de Bussy**

ARIADNE PRESS

Translated from the German *Kriminalfall Mayerling*
©1993 by Amalthea Verlag GmbH, Wien, München.

Library of Congress Cataloging-in-Publication Data

Markus, Georg.
    [Kriminalfall Mayerling. English]
    Crime at Mayerling : the life and death of mary vetsera :
with new expert opinions following the desecration of her grave /
Georg Markus ; translated by Carvel de Bussy.
        p.   cm. -- (Studies in Austrian literature, culture, and
    thought. Translation series)
    Includes bibliographical references and index.
    ISBN 0-929497-94-5
    1. Rudolf, Crown Prince of Austria, 1858-1889. 2. Vetsera,
Marie Alexandrine, Baronesse, 1871-1889. 3. Austria--Princes--
Biography. 4. Austria--Politics and government--1867-1917.
I. Title. II. Series.
DB89.R8M3713 1995
943.6'04--dc20   94-6491
                                                    CIP

Cover:
Designer, Art Director: George McGinnis

CONTENTS

FOREWORD

The word "Crime" in the title of this book has a double meaning. Crime Number One is history: the death of Crown Prince Rudolf and Baroness Mary Vetsera in 1889 at the hunting lodge at Mayerling. Crime Number Two takes place one hundred years later: a furniture dealer believes that he must solve the "riddle of Mayerling," opens a grave in the cemetery of Heiligenkreuz near Vienna and removes the remains of the Crown Prince's mistress.

The furniture dealer asserts that he purchased the skeleton, goes to newspapers and television companies, offering them the "story" of the stolen Mary Vetsera. The story appears to be so crazy that no one takes him seriously. When he came to me on December 1, 1992, I too could not believe the whole thing at first. Still, I checked the matter and after three weeks of research reached the conclusion that the businessman from Linz on the Danube really might have had the skeleton of Mary Vetsera. I reported a probable grave robbery to the public safety office in Vienna and thereupon a skeleton stored with a transfer and storage company in Vienna was secured by the police.

I wrote the story for my newspaper and it went around the world. Disseminated naturally by the media which had thought it so absurd that at first they wanted nothing to do with it.

Some things have happened since then. Following my report, the grave was opened on the authority of the public prosecutor in Vienna: It was empty!

The next step took place in February, 1993. Forensic doctors began the examination and analysis of the skeleton found in the grave, the skull, hair, clothing and shoes. These are the first results: There is no longer any doubt as to the identity of the remains: they are those of Mary Vetsera.

And when this book is published—before the forensic examinations are completed—the cause of her death can be regarded as settled. Contrary to early assumptions expressed

v

after the court-ordered seizure of the skeleton, it is now practically certain that Mary Vetsera was killed by a shot in the head.

This book is a mixture of historical reporting of the events at Mayerling, of the present crime, the personal experience of the author and the first medical conclusions that can be drawn since the grave robbery. People have puzzled, talked, written about the mystery of Mayerling for more than a hundred years. Today, for the first time, we are able to reconstruct with some precision how Baroness Vetsera died. It is the purpose of this book to help unravel the tragedy surrounding this important facet of the crime.

Vienna, March, 1993.   Georg MARKUS.

"I have already indicated during our telephone conversation that this is a sensation. You can believe me, Mr. Markus, I know your books and your historical articles, this is a story for you . . . "

"Let's get on with it, Mr. Flatzelsteiner."

"I am in possession of the skeleton of Mary Vetsera."

Idiot that I am, I am wasting my time here.

After that revelation, Mr. Flatzelsteiner sat back comfortably in his leather armchair. He probably thought that I should take out my pencil at once and write down every word. Such an imbecile! The waiter brought me a glass of mineral water.

I was not thinking of writing along. I was thinking of the appointments in the coming days. Interviews with Cardinal König, the celebrated physician Karl Fellinger, the cabaret artist Hugo Wiener, the indestructible Johannes Heesters. I wanted to write a story about these four men who, each of them eighty-eight years old, are still active in their professional lives. At eighty-eight! I was looking forward with pleasure to conversations with these four men who are admirable in every way.

And I am sitting here listening to the idiotic story of the stolen skeleton of Crown Prince Rudolf's mistress.

Flatzelsteiner continued with persistence. "I am offering you the story. We can agree on the price."

Yes, yes, naturally. But now here I am. I can cope with the ten minutes. "Mr. Flatzelsteiner, who can tell me that that there is something to this story you are giving me? You must admit that what you say is entirely unauthenticated!"

Flatzelsteiner admitted it.

And opened his red briefcase, taking out two folders of synthetic material. A brown one with the word "Fantasia" and a white one without label. Apparently they were folders containing some furniture collections with which this strange man might be acquainted.

But what had he to do with Austrian history? What did he want to know about a tragedy of this historical dimension? What did he want with Mayerling ?

3

"There Were Only Two Well-Aimed Shots"
The Night at Mayerling

January 30, 1889, caused indescribable horror throughout the world. Crown Prince Rudolf who, as future King of Austria-Hungary, was destined to guide the fate of a gigantic empire, died in a mysterious way in his hunting lodge at Mayerling near Vienna. Little else was reported at first. In the first reports there was no mention of violence nor anything about a second corpse.

The chamberlain Johann Loschek froze from terror on that ice-cold winter morning, when he discovered two dead persons in his master's bedroom: Archduke Rudolf, the thirty-year-old son of the Emperor of Austria, and Mary Vetsera, the daughter of a diplomat, not yet eighteen years old.

The valet later described the hours before and after the event as follows: "It was late in the evening when we all went to bed. But Rudolf and Mary did not sleep. I slept as usual in the next room and Rudolf said to me when we retired: 'You must let no one come to me, even the Emperor!' Vetsera was waiting for Rudolf in the room where she had eaten her last evening meal. All night long I heard Rudolf and Vetsera talking in very serious tones. I could not understand what they said. At about 6:10 in the morning Rudolf came out to me in the room completely dressed and ordered me to hitch up the horses. I had not come to the courtyard yet when I heard two detonations; I ran back at once and met the smell of powder. I raced to the bedroom but, contrary to habit, it was locked. Otherwise, Rudolf never locked the room. What should I do? I called Count Hoyos at once (Note: the Crown Prince's hunting partner) and knocked in the door panel with a hammer, so that I could get my hand inside to unlock the door. What a dreadful sight! Rudolf lay dead upon his bed, fully dressed. Mary Vetsera likewise on her bed, completely dressed. Rudolf's army revolver lay beside him. Both had not slept at all. Both of their heads hung down. At the first glance, one

4

could see that Rudolf had first shot Mary Vetsera and then killed himself. There were only two well-aimed shots. The presence of a third person, as well as that fragments of glass were sticking in Rudolf's head, has just been made up, like too much about Rudolf's death . . . . "

There was a note on the Crown Prince's night table on which stood these words: "Dear Loschek! Fetch a priest and have us buried together in the same grave at Heiligenkreuz. Bring my dear Mary's jewelry with her letter to Mary's mother. I thank you for your service which was always so faithful and devoted over the many years you spent with me. Send the letter to my wife immediately. Rudolf."

Loshek collapsed after reading these words. "I knelt down and laid my head on Rudolf's arm and cried bitterly . . . We brought Rudolf's body to Baden on that same day, arriving at nine o'clock in the evening. Porters carried the coffin to a Pullman car and only I and Dr. Widerhofer (Note: the Imperial physician) accompanied our good lord to Vienna."

These lines, which the chamberlain, now 83 years old, dictated to his son in 1928, nearly forty years after Mayerling, constitute the only direct testimony from the site of the event. Of course, their credibility will be at least partially questioned by historians. For example, it has been shown that the door of the Crown Prince's bedroom was not broken open "at once," but not until two hours after the fact, and that Mary was not dressed at the time of her death. During the night she had taken off her tight-fitting, olive green suit with the black lace. The dark red felt hat with ostrich feathers, the boa and the veil also lay scattered on the armchairs of the bedroom and her shoes stood beside the bed.

The often-mentioned "Mystery of Mayerling" could not be resolved for an entire century principally because the death of Crown Prince Rudolf and especially that of Baroness Mary Vetsera—in contrast with any other crime—were never seriously investigated. And the few investigations that were made were hushed up, falsified and manipulated by the Royal House.

Otherwise the following striking, unexplained contradictions would be inconceivable:

1. Loschek asserted that he had informed Count Hoyos immediately after 6:10 when he heard the shots. But Hoyos stated that he was not called until eight o'clock.

2. The chamberlain told Count Hoyos that Rudolf and Mary died from potassium cyanide. How could he then have heard two detonations?

3. Count Hoyos took the train to Vienna, in order to inform the Emperor of the tragedy. Whereas he had a fast train stopped at the Baden railway station, indicating that "the Crown Prince has shot himself," he reported an hour later to the Emperor that Rudolf was poisoned by Baroness Vetsera. The public did not hear either version immediately after the event. The official "Wiener Zeitung" spoke on 31 January 1889 of the Crown Prince's suffering a "heart attack." Still, in spite of strict censorship, this manipulated report could not be long maintained.

The wildest rumors circulated in all parts of the Monarchy precisely because newspapers that wrote against the "official version" were confiscated. People talked about an orgy at which Rudolf was struck down with a champagne bottle. There was whispering of a hunting accident and of a jealous game-keeper who shot Rudolf because the Crown Prince had allegedly seduced his wife. Others said that after falling from a horse, Rudolf suffered such severe headaches that he took his own life because of that. From a political point of view, the German Chancellor Bismarck, the Frenchman Clemenceau, the Freemasons, the Jews and the Hungarians were the targets of suspicion. The last, because the Crown Prince rejected the Crown of St. Stephen which he was said to have already accepted.

the skeleton of an eighteen-year-old who died on 1 May 1889 . . . no, not the eighteen-year-old Mary Vetsera . . . , but the eighteen-year-old Theresia Vindona.

"Mr. Flatzelsteiner," I said, with an impatient glance at the time, "Mr. Flatzelsteiner, what interest do I have in this Theresia Vindona, who allegedly died 'from a shot or a knife wound' (Note: quoted from Professor Szilvássy's report)? This was undoubtedly a tragic case. But I ask you, what am I supposed to do with it after more than a hundred years?"

Mr. Flatzelsteiner took me into his confidence. "There never was a Theresia Vindona. I said that she was my great grandmother. I could not say that it was the skeleton of Mary Vetsera. What do you imagine would have happened then!"

So, he could not tell it to the forensic doctor. But he could tell it to me. How did I get into this, letting my time be taken up?

I had scarcely returned the report to Mr. Flatzelsteiner—because it did not interest me, as any sensible person will understand—when the fellow from Linz began excitedly to fumble around in his folder. This furniture dealer, who did not in any way seem to be insane, but who was probably not quite normal either, was obviously afraid (as I can imagine now) that after ORF, RTL, Bunte . . . and whoever else, that another journalist would desert him before knowing what this was really about.

Mr. Flatzelsteiner turned to page four of the Szilvássy report. "Summary: The data agree with the statements of the client, Mr. Helmut Flatzelsteiner. The skeleton which has been examined is that of an eighteen-year-old female with a height of five feet four inches. It has lain in the ground for about one-hundred years . . . ."

I could see from the photographs that the said girl had especially long hair (it was still there) and that her clothing was that of a young lady "of the better class." On one picture which was a bit faded one could even read the label of the store where the garment had been purchased: "Josef Fischer, Tailor to the Royal Court, Tailor for Horsewomen, English Clothing for Gentlemen and Ladies and Liveries. Vienna I., Lobko-witzplatz 1, Mezzanine."

So it was clear: This man in front of me had a skeleton which had been examined by forensic medical officials. They were the remains of a woman whose characteristics corresponded strikingly with all of those I knew of Mary Vetsera: Mary died 100 years ago, she was eighteen, had long hair and was rather short. And the clothes might also resemble those of a young noblewoman in the era of the Ringstrasse.

Still: The story was too crazy.

"Well, what do you say?" Flatzelsteiner asked.

One must be careful with such people. Who knows? They might be violent. There was nobody else in the hotel hall besides us two. Even the waiter had long ago disappeared.

"Striking parallels," I said. "But how do you conclude that these could be the remains of Vetsera? Here it says Theresia Vindona. Nothing else. "Where did you get the body?" I asked. And I was surprised at myself that I was willing to pursue this clearly crazy matter.

"I bought it," Flatzelsteiner said.

"Bought? From whom?"

"It is a long story, I shall tell you the next time. Only this much: Mary Vetsera was stolen from her grave in Heiligenkreuz at the request of an aristocrat by two people from Burgenland (Note: a federal Austrian state opposite the Hungarian frontier). The aristocrat did not pay, so the two sat there with their skeleton and offered it to me. I bought it for thirty-thousand schillings."

O God! What nonsense! "Mr. Flatzelsteiner, I'll think it over. You will hear from me." Flatzelsteiner with his red case took the train back to Linz; I went by car to my apartment in Vienna.

I thought about it during the trip. If the fellow really has a skeleton which has so much in common with all we know about Mary Vetsera, then maybe it is really the right one. Those two people possibly from Burgenland, or whoever they were, would have had to open a hundred graves until they found a skeleton of a girl who died a hundred years ago at eighteen, was short in height and had long hair. So it would have been simpler to steal the real Mary Vetsera than so many with that personal description.

When leaving him, I took down the telephone number of Mr. Flatzelsteiner's lawyer, Dr. Johannes Worm, likewise in Linz. Oh my, I thought at once. If that is the brother of Alfred Worm, the journalist and scandal-monger of the country, and if there is really something in this Vetsera thing, then Worm will of course hear about it and the story will appear in his newspaper.

Obviously, the story is only interesting if one gets it first and exclusive. But first there was still no idea that there could be anything in it.

A telephone call to Dr. Worm in Linz. "Tell me, Doctor, what is this with Mr. Flatzelsteiner? Is he all right? I mean . . . , you know . . . ?"

Dr. Worm was surprised. "He is a serious businessman. Whatever he does is okay."

"And this story about the stolen Mary Vetsera?"

"I only know about it from what he tells me, but when Mr. Flatzelsteiner says it, there is something to it, I am sure."

He said that if there were a contract about the exclusive reporting, he would handle it.

Later that evening, I looked through the biography of Mary Vetsera. In fact, the Crown Prince's mistress had been buried with the clothes she wore on the evening before her death at Mayerling. An olive green suit with black lace, a felt hat, a boa, stockings and also the shoes . . . that could all correspond entirely with the contents of the grave shown on the pictures that Flatzelsteiner had shown me.

A few days later I had a meeting with Hans Dichand, the publisher and editor-in-chief of my newspaper. The door to the "sanctum sanctorum" on the eleventh floor of the Vienna press building was always open to its editors. I know some (much smaller) newspapers whose staff see the editor-in-chief once or twice a year, at Christmastime or at a time of crisis.

People can see Hans Dichand any day, if they have something to tell him.

And I had something to tell him. But for Heaven's sake, what? Mary Vetsera's body stolen from the grave, a certain Mr. Flatzelsteiner as informant . . .

The old fox sat beside me, his eyes wide open. If anyone knows what a story is, he is the one. Hans Dichand made every newspaper he managed one of the largest in the country. First, the *Kleine Zeitung* at Graz, then the *Kurier* and now the *Kronen Zeitung*.

"It might be something," he said, being just as skeptical as I, and equally fascinated by the thought that there could be something to it. That is what is strange about our profession: all of us reject violence, corruption and crime and still we know that it all exists, has always existed and always will. All newspapers live from the scandals of the world and want to be the first to report them. No reasonable physician wants his patients to be sick and yet he needs their illnesses to practice his profession. A truly paradoxical situation in which we journalists also find ourselves.

Hence my fear that Dr. Worm might be the brother of Alfred Worm. If Mary Vetsera's grave had in fact been desecrated, we must be the first to write about it.

But we were still far away from that, for what we had in our hands was still insufficient.

A call to Mr. Flatzelsteiner, second meeting, this time in the editorial office. It was December 9th. The informant again had brought his red case. "Tell us, Mr. Flatzelsteiner, tell us! These two people from Burgenland, how was that exactly? When did you make contact with them and where?"

It just came out with a gush. Flatzelsteiner was glad to finally get rid of his story. I knew that this man from Linz was a bit nervous. But it was also quite an adventure he had to report, if it is true . . .

"So, it was in a dance hall called the "Slovanka Split" at Budweis. There I met the two of them."

"When, exactly?"

14

"I do not remember quite exactly. But it must . . . "

"Mr. Flatzelsteiner, think back carefully."

"It must have been four years ago."

"1988? When, more precisely!"

"In the spring."

He said the two from Burgenland visited him later at his furniture store in Linz and revealed to him for the first time that the dead person was Mary Vetsera. When asked for proof of their statement, the two thieves gave him a pair of shoes. Mr. Flatzelsteiner took them to his neighbor, Erich Hagendorfer, head of the shoemakers' union for Upper Austria, who confirmed that the shoes were about a hundred years old. "Now I thought it was more likely that this was Mary Vetsera's body," said Flatzelsteiner. Later the two men delivered to him the skeleton together with the coffin and items of clothing, for which he paid them 30,000 schillings.

It was clear to Flatzelsteiner from the start that if the remains were genuine, he would return them to their legal owner, the monastery at Heiligenkreuz. In any case, that was the version he gave me.

I thought about what to do next. The *Kronen Zeitung* would have to make a contract with Mr. Flatzelsteiner. We should have to have the skeleton examined by forensic doctors and—this was quite important—make a report to the police prior to the first publication about the suspicion of a grave robbery. And inform the Abbot of Heiligenkreuz at the same time. I was certain that this was not just any story, but a crime in which I was involved as a newspaperman and also as a citizen who had to carry out his duty with respect to the authorities.

Mary's Death's Head on My Desk
Professor Bankl Is Brought In

Hans Dichand agreed with all the steps I suggested. He gave me a free hand to act as I thought proper. Of course, I still kept constantly in touch with his office, with him, with Dr. Friedrich Dragon and Willi Haunold. They were the first I had informed of the "Mary Vetsera Case".

But I knew that the circle had to grow larger. Because we newspapermen could never determine alone whether Mr. Flatzelsteiner in fact had the remains of Vetsera in his possession. Or whether this was a colossal fraud.

I always had the "Hitler Diaries" in mind as an example. In April, 1983, reporters of the illustrated magazine *Stern* announced the exclusive publication of the "Führer's" notes which had just been discovered. Now, history would have to be rewritten, as they demanded. And thereby they caused the journalistic bankruptcy of the century. For the diaries had been written later on and turned out to be the ingenious trick of a forger named Konrad Kujau. Experts of the German Federal Archives clearly proved that the paper, ink and paste all came from the postwar period.

Sleepless nights. Was this Flatzelsteiner a second Kujau? On the other hand: a diary can be forged. But a skeleton? Impossible! And there were the expert opinions whose authenticity was beyond doubt.

We needed a specialist here who was an expert in pathology and forensic medicine and was also acquainted with the historical circumstances and the life and death of Baroness Vetsera. For me, there was only one who met all these criteria. His name is Hans Bankl, who is professor of pathological anatomy at the University of Vienna and has already written a book on the *Illnesses and Death of Historical Personalities*, including a chapter on Mary and Rudolf. But I could not take him into my confidence, especially not him.

There was a prologue to the affair and Mary Vetsera played

one of the main parts in it. I had known Bankl for several years. My first big story about him came out in March, 1987. By small detective work, the professor obtained bone fragments of Ludwig van Beethoven which had been "removed" at the time of a transfer of his mortal remains thirty-five years after the death of the musical genius. Bankl made contact with a descendant of the Vienna doctor Romeo Seligmann, who had taken three pieces of bone at the time of the exhumation of Beethoven in 1863 from his celebrated head. And in fact Seligmann's great grandnephew Thomas Desmines still had the pieces of the head from his uncle's collection after more than a hundred years and gave them to Bankl, who was able to determine the cause of Beethoven's deafness on the basis of that sensational find. It was not—as doctors had all assumed throughout the world—due to the bone disease called "Mordus Paget," but rather to an otosclerosis of the inner ear, an early ossification of the auditory system.

I got along well with Bankl. He was one of those scientists who knew—in all seriousness—what interests newspaper readers. And he always found something new, interesting, sensational. During our conversation about Beethoven—he had also written a book about the case together with his colleague Hans Jesserer—Bankl mentioned another sensational project that he wanted to prepare. Dr. Bankl intended to have the remains of Mary Vetsera exhumed. At that time, in March, 1987, five and a half years before Flatzelsteiner, I had been confronted with Crown Prince Rudolf's mistress. With this fine distinction: Whereas Flatzelsteiner was giving me a "robber story," which was to go around the world, it undoubtedly began with criminal action, while Bankl was thinking about the serious action of a team of scientists which intended to find the trace of the often-cited "Mayerling Puzzle."

Today we know that the "robber story" did what science was unable to accomplish. And I was not entirely free of blame for this. Thus it was impossible to bring Professor Bankl into the "Mary Vetsera Case."

I had not heard from Bankl for one and a half years.

17

Suddenly, he called up. He said that now everything was ready. He had obtained approval from the Abbot of the Heiligenkreuz monastery and from the two great grandnieces of Mary Vetsera who were still alive. Hence, nothing more seemed to stand in the way of the exhumation to be performed by a team of pathologists and forensic doctors.

Except a sum of money amounting to 40,000 schillings. If the *Kronen Zeitung* made this money available—it only covered the costs of the stonemasons, pallbearers and other assistants, for the doctors would not ask for honoraria—then the paper could have exclusive coverage of the results of the exhumation for its readers.

It is true that Hans Dichand approved of this at that time. But everything turned out differently in that autumn of 1988 and, as it was learned later, played an important part in the story of the grave robbery in 1992.

Everything happened differently, for shortly after Bankl's okay a medical publishing house called me to say that we could not get by with forty-thousand schillings; according to the latest calculation, it would come to one-hundred-thousand.

My newspaper would have been willing to pay that, but a few days later I received a telephone call from a "press agent" in Munich, Count Something-or-Other, who said that the one-hundred-thousand would be insufficient, at least in schillings. All right if the entire amount were paid in German marks.

This was strong stuff. Support for a scientific project was turning into big business. I knew from the start that Professor Bankl had nothing to do with these sordid machinations. A few men had smuggled themselves into the project, hoping to make a small fortune from the exhumation of Mary Vetsera. They wanted brazenly to exploit Dr. Bankl's idea.

Another call from the "agent." He said the *Illustrated* was willing to pay the price recently asked. A German revolver publication asked me to write a special contribution about the planned exhumation of Mary. I had kept the matter to myself for one and a half years; we had a (verbal) exclusive contract with Dr. Bankl, but meanwhile the project had made such large waves that I no longer felt any reason to observe the agreement on silence, since in any case half the news industry was already aware of it.

It was November 3, 1988. In order to get ahead of other newspapers, I wrote this headline in the *Krone*: "Mary Vetsera's Grave to Be Opened." The results were dramatic. Both the Abbot of Heiligenkreuz and the Vetsera descendents withdrew the agreement which had already been made, saying that the exhumation was to be made "solely for scientific purposes."

A few weeks later "Club 2" of Austrian Television brought out "Mayerling 100 Years Ago." During the talk show, Bankl accused me of having impeded his project by revealing it to the public prematurely. The following day, I corrected his charges in the newspaper, reported on the "agent" and others who wanted to profit from this scientific project and said that it was because of their irresponsible activity that it had failed.

Almost three years later, Mr. Flatzelsteiner was here with "his" Mary. I needed an expert. I knew none better than Bankl. But we had fallen out with each other since January, 1989.

Nevertheless I telephoned him. I breathed a sigh of relief: Bankl was friendly and willing to talk. I did not say anything concrete on the telephone, only: "I have learned something important. Should like to meet you."

Thursday, December 17, 1992. Two meetings, one after the other. 2:30 P.M. Mr. Flatzelsteiner arrived at the editorial office and opened his red case. He took out all kinds of papers, photographs—I was already acquainted with all of that. And suddenly: a death's head. "That is Mary" Flatzelsteiner said.

When my colleague Connie Bischofberger asked me later in an interview how I felt when Mary's skull was lying on my desk, I said: "I was physically ill at ease."

But Flatzelsteiner had not come on that December 17, 1992, solely because of Mary's head, but also to sign a contract. The *Kronen Zeitung* obtained the right to exclusive publication of the story about the theft of Mary Vetsera's remains and would therefor assume the costs of the forensic examinations made up to then (eighty-thousand schillings).

Thirty minutes later, appointment with Professor Bankl in Hans Dichand's office. The contract with Flatzelsteiner had to be signed before then, in order to take over from him the forensic medical opinions and the photographs. The contract would have become invalid if it was learned that the dead person was clearly not Mary. Above all, if it were found upon opening the grave that Baroness Vetsera was still lying there.

I tried to prepare Bankl carefully. "Professor, this is a crazy story. Someone is claiming . . . And I recited the Flatzelsteiner version to him.

Bankl looked from Hans Dichand to me and back again. "That cannot be true, it is impossible."

I unpacked the expert opinions of his colleagues Szilvássy and Jarosch. The expertise of Dr. Michael Stolz, the dental surgeon in Linz. The clothing examinations and the photographs of the skeleton, skull, hair, shoes, clothing . . .

Bankl could not believe his eyes. He shook his head, read the opinions carefully, looked at the photographs. Did not say a word. Dichand and I waited entranced. I could not stand it any longer. "So, Professor, what do you think of the whole affair?"

"I could imagine," and he emphasized every single word, "I could imagine that . . . " and he paused in a highly interesting dramatic way, " . . . I could imagine that it is genuine!"

"You think it is possible that the skeleton of the real Mary Vetsera was stolen, examined and photographed?"

"Yes, I think so!"

The Vetsera discovery could turn out to be a sensation. It was possible that we were on the way to solving part of the Mayerling puzzle.—Or the historians would face a still greater puzzle in the future than they had up to now.

When Bankl had left, Dichand took me aside and said: "Who knows whether this Flatzelsteiner did not open the grave himself!"

"I do not think so," I replied. After the three or four conversations I had with the furniture dealer from Linz, I should not have thought him capable of such a deed.

"I Must Do Everything He Asks of Me"
The Short Life of Mary Vetsera

Who was the young woman whose remains had been allegedly stolen from her grave at Heiligenkreuz? People did not know very much about the life and death of the girl, since at that time the Imperial Court in Vienna did everything possible to conceal what had occurred during the few years which it was given for this blossoming creature to live.

Marie Alexandrine Freiin von Vetsera was born on March 19, 1871, in Vienna as the third of four children of the diplomat Albin Vetsera, of Bratislava and Helene née Baltazzi. The King of Prussia, Wilhelm I, was proclaimed Emperor of Germany at Versailles in the year that she was born; the Prime Minister of Hungary and former revolutionary Count Gyula Andrássy became the Foreign Minister of Austria-Hungary, and the metric system of weights and measures was introduced by law in the monarchy. The Suez Canal and the Vienna Court Opera were opened two years before her birth. The "golden operettas" of Johann Strauss and Jacques Offenbach were at their height when she was a child.

At first, "Mary," as she was soon called, lived in her parents' villa located at Am Schüttel 11 in the Viennese Leopoldstadt, before the family moved to the more elegant Palais Vetsera, later Palais Salm, at Salesianergasse 11. First, Mary Vetsera was taught by private instructors at home and later attended the "Institute for Daughters of the Nobility" at the Salesian monastery, where she was to be prepared for "life in the big world."

Mary was what was known as a "good Imperial mixture" (eine gute Kaisermischung). Her paternal ancestors were Slavs and Germans, her mother's Italians, Greeks and Englishmen. Mary's parents had met in Constantinople, where Albin Vetsera was then secretary in the Austrian Embassy. Mary's mother, who was just sixteen when she was married, came from a family of wealthy bankers with business in the East. Albin

Vetsera, twenty-two years older than his wife, had originally been a friend of her parents and after their premature death was appointed guardian of all ten Baltazzi children. In 1864, he married his eldest ward. It was anything but a love marriage. Helene was looked upon rather as a "good match." Apparently the marriage with one of the richest girls of Constantinople was advantageous for Albin's career: he very quickly became minister plenipotentiary at St. Petersburg, Lisbon and at the Hessian Court. Through her father, who was named baron (Freiherr) by Emperor Francis Joseph in 1870, belonging to the lower nobility, and possessing immense wealth from her mother's family, Mary was soon circulating in the best circles of the capital. Since the father was sickly and because of his profession was often abroad, the mother, well-known for her gaiety, held many wild parties in her salon. Being herself a first-class rider, she did not miss any horse race and was a welcome guest at elegant dinners, soirées and balls. One of the ladies-in-waiting of Empress Elisabeth wrote in her diary in 1877: "Madame Vetsera wants to come to Court and gain recognition for her family."

And one reads in the *Wiener Salonblatt* that Helene Vetsera "shows great interest in the public life of the Residence and rarely misses a banquet."

Mary's uncle Hector Baltazzi was a successful jockey; Alexander and Aristides, two other brothers of her mother, brought horses from their own stables to international races. In 1876 they won the Epsom Derby in the presence of Queen Victoria against overpowering English competition. But the brothers also had a legendary reputation as politicians, officers and men of the world who were always present at important affairs in London, Paris, St. Petersburg and Vienna. Heinrich Baltazzi, the youngest of the four brothers, was known as the "most elegant gentleman in the Monarchy" and was mentioned by Arthur Schnitzler as "the unrivaled image of an ideal, Henry Baltazzi, whom I later met and who thus became the model for the count in *Reigen*."

Mary had her first encounter with death when she was ten.

On December 8, 1881, her elder brother Ladislaus, who had gone to a staging of *The Tales of Hoffmann*, did not return home. The sixteen-year-old cadet in a military school was one of the victims of the fire at the Ring Theater, where altogether three-hundred and eighty-six persons died. One and a half years before the catastrophe at Mayerling, Mary's father died at the age of sixty-two in Cairo after a stroke.

According to Marie Nunziante, the owner of a dress salon in Vienna, the seventeen-year-old Baroness had "a charming figure, and one cannot imagine how sweet her head was. Her complexion tended towards brown, she had wonderfully fresh cheeks, almond-shaped eyes and black hair. One was happy just to look at her." In the Vetsera biography in the records of the family solicitor, Hermann Swistun, she is described as "mature before her years, with a perfect figure, a small snub nose above a small red mouth; her eyes were deep blue and unusually large." Of course, her education, like that of girls of a higher class, was complete. She had no intellectual pretensions and, besides her clothes, was only interested in ice skating and the racetrack.

And there it was, at a race in Freudenau, that she saw Crown Prince Rudolf for the first time on April 12, 1888, in the Court loge, from rather close up. Mary left behind in a diary entry that "a passion was born" on that afternoon, and Princess Nora Fugger noted in her memoirs that the Crown Prince "seemed to have agreed with Mary's look, and that turned her head entirely."

Gabriel Dubray, Mary's French teacher, described the last months of his pupil's life in an article for the Paris *Matin*: "In the spring of 1888 the Baroness appeared to have fallen in love with the Crown Prince, for from then on there was a noticeable change in her attitude and mood. She spoke about him with great enthusiasm, but I thought the matter harmless. I hoped it would evaporate when once a serious suitor presented himself to the pretty girl who was then seventeen."

The "serious suitor" appeared precisely at that time. Obviously as a result of an intensive campaign by Mary's extremely ambitious mother, Miguel de Braganza, who was serving in the Austro-Hungarian army, began to pay active attention to the young baroness. However, even when associating with the widowed Portuguese duke, who was a close hunting companion of Rudolf's, she was only interested in one thing: to learn everything about the Austrian Crown Prince, whom she adored. Like so many teenagers of that time, Mary collected photographs and newspaper clippings of Rudolf, about whose unhappy marriage all Vienna was talking. When her chambermaid Agnes Jahoda, whom she had taken into her confidence, tried to talk her out of her rapturous passion for the Emperor's son, Mary only said: "I swear that I shall never love anyone else!"

Mary spent the summer of 1888—the last vacation of her life—traveling with her mother and sisters through England, France and Germany, where the ladies always entertained in an elegant manner. Even the Prince of Wales, England's later King Edward VII, came to the "Villa Imperiale" that Helene Vetsera rented at Bad Homburg. Mary became friends there with an American, Maureen Alleen, who later recalled: "The Baroness looked charming, was highly approved by society, but was very serious. Although unselfish in her manner, people gave her credit for not taking love lightly, but rather quite seriously and tragically, if it became necessary."

Apparently it became "necessary." For Mary had hardly returned to Vienna in the beginning of September when she sent a fanciful letter to Rudolf, audaciously suggesting that she wanted to meet him in person.

The message reached the Emperor's son just as he had arrived at a low point in his life. The Court was expecting Germany's new ruler, Wilhelm II, whom Rudolf detested, for his first state visit to Vienna. Wilhelm's accession to the throne had been a severe blow for Rudolf, who had hoped for a liberal alliance with his father and predecessor, Friedrich III. Upon Friedrich's unexpectedly early death, the Austrian Crown Prince's ideal of a European future directed towards peace collapsed. While Rudolf had no hope of acceding to the throne in the foreseeable future, his adversary Wilhelm had come to power.

The Crown Prince knew that Wilhelm's policy aimed entirely at military confrontation and so he urged non-renewal of the alliance with Germany which would expire in the coming year, in order to seek a peaceful solution of the Balkan problems with Russia which had been postponed. As in so many political questions, the Crown Prince's suggestion fell on deaf ears with the Emperor, who held fast to his foreign policy oriented towards Prussia. While the new German Emperor was in Vienna, Rudolf made a point of going hunting with the Prince of Wales in Siebenbürgen. Rudolf could not have expressed his distaste for Wilhelm more clearly than in a letter he mailed from there to his wife Stephanie. He said: "I was glad to invite (the Prince of) Wales; I should invite Wilhelm only to get him out of this world through a hunting accident."

It was precisely in these days which were so depressing for him that Rudolf answered the teenager Mary in a registered letter for general delivery as she had asked. He said that he also had a "lively desire" to talk with her. He suggested a meeting in the Prater (park)(Note: but they met in the Hofburg). He told her she should give any further correspondence to his valet Loschek.

Pleased with this response, Mary asked Marie Louise Larisch to go with her as chaperon. Countess Larisch was a friend of Mary's mother and a niece of the Empress. She came from the morganatic marriage of Duke Ludwig in Bavaria—Elisabeth's older brother—with the former actress Henriette Mendel. She was allowed to call herself Baroness Wallersee until she married Count Georg Larisch. She lived with him in Pardubitz in Bohemia, but often came to Vienna, where she stayed at the Grand Hotel on the Ring Strasse. And so it was on November 5, 1888, when, thanks to her assistance, there was the first meeting between Mary and Rudolf.

Mary wrote of this first meeting to her confidante Hermine Tobis, her former piano teacher, who was living in Frankfurt am Main: "Today you are receiving a very happy letter, because I met him. Marie Larisch took me with her to run some errands; then we went to the "Adele" (studio) to be photographed, for him, of course, and then we went behind the Grand Hotel where Bratfisch was waiting for us. We hid our faces tightly in our boas and there we went at full gallop into the Burg. An old valet was waiting for us at a small iron door and he led us up several dark stairs and through some rooms; finally, he stopped in front of a door and had us go in . . . A voice called out from a neighboring room: "Please, ladies, come on in. I am here!" We entered, Marie introduced me, and we fell at once into a Viennese conversation . . . When we left he (Note: the Crown Prince) led us himself through a large, dark room and over a stairs and said to Marie: "Please! Bring her to me soon again!"

The letter ended with these words: "Hermine, you must swear to me to say nothing about this letter to anyone, neither to Hanna (Mary's sister) nor Mother, for if one of those two ever learned of it, I should have to kill myself."

On the way home, Mary spoke about the Crown Prince in the carriage of Rudolf's personal driver, Josef Bratfisch, saying to Countess Larisch: "He was just as adorable as I had imagined."

Three months of happiness followed, with many secret meetings, nearly always arranged by Marie Larisch.

An embarrassing incident occurred during one of the first of them. It was described by Police Inspector Friedrich Heide in a report to the Chief of Police after the events at Mayerling. "In late autumn of last year Countess Larisch and Baroness Vetsera drove to the Prater and the Crown Prince followed. Both carriages met up with the Crown Princess. Her Highness drove after them and met them in the Krieau." Blunders of that kind by her husband had long been nothing new for Rudolf's wife Stephanie.

From the beginning, the disparate lovers shared a melancholy longing for death. Of course, their motives were quite different. Whereas the lack of a political alternative and his personal and medical problems were determining factors for Rudolf, Mary only thought of death because she saw that a lasting relationship with her beloved "in this life" was impossible. She once said "if I could give him my life, I should be glad to do it, for what does life mean for me?" "We have made a pact relative to that possibility. If it came to that, in some place that no one knows, after some happy hours, we should die together."

Mary's mother said in a memorandum she published after the death, that there was no reason for alarm because of her "idolizing devotion, the charm of his physical presence and the Crown Prince's chivalrous nature and Mary's age, which was almost that of a child, and in addition the lack of any personal contact."[1]

Of course, there was less "lack" of personal contact than in Helene Vetsera's information about it. Her daughter's meetings with the Crown Prince took place in greatest secrecy. Usually Mary went to the Hofburg—driven by Bratfisch—when her mother was engaged in her numerous social activities. Rudolf's close friend Count Josef Hoyos, left us among his papers an example of the tricks Mary used in order to meet her lover. "She avoided having to go to the theater one evening by washing her hair, presenting herself to her mother, who scolded her roundly. She remarked that she thought her hair would soon be dry, but since that was not the case, she could not possibly go with them to the theater and so would have to stay at home." Mother and sister had scarcely left the house when Mary hurried to Bratfisch, whose carriage was waiting a short distance from her house, in the Marokkanergasse, to take her to the Hofburg.

Besides Countess Larisch, only her chambermaid Agnes and her piano teacher Hermine Tobis shared Mary's great

---

[1] Helene Vetsera's memorandum was confiscated by the Imperial authorities and stamped; it appeared later in foreign publications.

secret. She wrote to the latter at Frankfurt am Main on January 14, 1889: Dear Hermine, today I must confess to you something that will make you very angry. I was with him yesterday from seven to eight. We both lost our heads. Now we belong to each other in body and soul."

There is no doubt that the evening of January 13th, mentioned in her letter, was a special day for Mary. Not alone because she had underlined the date in red in her diary (as she always did when she met the Crown Prince). She said to her chambermaid after her return; "Ah, Agnes, it would have been much better if I had not gone out today." Nevertheless, she was "grateful to Fate, for now I no longer belong to myself alone, but only to him. From now on I must do everything he asks of me."

Even though Helene Vetsera knew nothing of her daughter's relationship with the son of the Austrian Emperor, she could have suspected it. At least after the story of the tabatière. Two days after the "special" January 13th, Mary purchased a golden cigarette box from the exclusive firm Rodek Brothers, purveyors to the Court on the Kohlmarkt in Vienna, in which she had the words "January 13. Thanks to Fate" (13. Janner. Dank dem Schicksal) engraved. She was accompanied by a lady companion. Shortly before that purchase, she had received a large sum of money from her uncle and guardian Alexander Baltazzi. Although she tried to convince her companion that she wanted to give the case to one of her uncles, the next day, during another ride through the Prater, she gave the valuable present to her beloved Crown Prince.

Naturally there are various speculations about what happened on that ominous January 13, 1889, so shortly before the catastrophe at Mayerling. It is certain that what took place in those days had far-reaching consequences for Mary and Rudolf. While many biographers think that was the time of their sexual union, others believe that their decision on joint suicide was taken on that day. On the other hand, Gerd Holler, a physician and Mayerling specialist, is convinced that "a one hundred percent confirmation of pregnancy came on that

January 13th".

In any case, the lady companion who accompanied Mary to the Rodek Brothers on the Kohlmarkt informed her mother of the "suspicious" purchase. Hermann Swistun, the administrator of the estate, stated: "When she was vigorously questioned by her mother, Mary admitted that she had sent the cigarette case anonymously to the Crown Prince as a compliment. Then, after intense reproof, the girl had to open her jewelry case which was always locked, where the mother found another, iron cigarette case engraved with Rudolf's monogram, some young and childhood pictures of the Prince and Mary's will, drawn up on January 18th."

Helene Vetsera was beside herself and thought first of all of the threatening scandal, if it were to be known that it was her daughter who was making advances to the married Crown Prince. "She is compromising herself when she is scarcely seventeen years old and so is ruining not only her own life but also that of her brothers and sisters and her mother if the Crown Prince and his people learn who sent him the gift. And what is the origin of that iron cigarette case with the monogram?"

With tears in her eyes, Mary declared that she had received the iron case as a present from Countess Larisch, because she was so enthusiastic about the Crown Prince. She said the Countess had received it as a gift from her cousin Rudolf. On the other hand, she said she had made the will, because she had a presentiment that perhaps she would not grow old and that through an illness or accident she would not be able to preserve her short lifeline. Since in her testament Mary bequeathed mainly pieces of jewelry to sisters, aunts and women friends, her mother considered the matter as nonsense and a young girl's exaggeration. As Agnes was also mentioned in the will, the mother also questioned her closely as to whether she knew anything about the tobacco boxes or the will. This she denied (keeping her word, which she had given Mary: author's note)."

Mary and Rudolf went to Mayerling on January 28, 1889.

The road to the catastrophe had long since been prepared.

"The Grave Is Empty!"
No Second "Hitler Diaries"

"I could imagine that it is genuine." These words of the pathologist Dr. Hans Bankl were the starting gun for the "Mary Vetsera Case." Hans Dichand and I suggested to the doctor that he ought to examine the remains very carefully before we made the story public. He agreed in principle, but he felt that he had to inform Professors Georg Bauer, head of the Institute for Forensic Medicine in Vienna, and Johann Szilvássy of the matter. Bankl would support our plan of having the authenticity of the alleged skeleton of Baroness Vetsera tested together with his colleagues.

So we remained in agreement that he would contact the two gentlemen. Later on Friday afternoon Professor Bankl said that his colleagues Bauer and Szilvássy would need time to think about it over the weekend. I should have the answer on Monday morning.

Monday, December 21, 1992, 10 A.M. Professor Georg Bauer on the telephone: "I have thought it over carefully, Mr. Markus. We cannot do it that way. If these are really the remains of an individual of such great historical significance, I must report it to my superiors in the Ministry of Science."

For me, this was an entirely new situation. By so doing, there would clearly be too many persons in on the secret. At this stage, the story was already "too hot." We had to make it public, could not wait any longer. If anyone leaked it now, the story was dead. I asked Professor Bauer to give me twenty-four hours head start and he agreed.

I called Willi Haunold at the editorial office: "We must start the Mary Vetsera story immediately. Today!"

"Impossible!" he replied. "A lot is going on today. Airplane accident over Portugal with one-hundred and fifty dead. Shock in the West: Serbian President Slobodan Milošević has had an electoral victory over his challenger Milan Panić. I have no space for an opener nor for an inside page!"

I explained that the story was threatening to blow up unless we put it out at once. Whereupon Haunold "shoveled" page 1 and 8/9 free for the evening edition.

It was nearly 2 P.M. when I called Hofrat Max Edelbacher, head of the Public Safety Bureau in Vienna. I said that I had to make a report today about a sensational case to which I cautiously referred as "a kind of art theft." So I should come to meet him at about 5 P.M. In doing this I was thinking that our newspaper would be on the streets by 5:30. The police had to know the story of the theft of Mary Vetsera's remains (which was still conjectural then), but not learn of it from the newspaper, rather prior to its publication and from myself. On the other hand, I dared not make the report too soon, because the report would pass from the press office of the Chief of Police to all of the media.

Besides that, I still had to write the story during the afternoon which we were to publish—naturally exclusive—in the evening. The first (of altogether seven) *Krone* headlines on this subject in the first ten days after the event became known ran: "Mary Vetsera Stolen from the Grave".

At 4:40 P.M. I was sitting in the Public Safety office across from its chief, Hofrat Edelbacher, the lawyer Dr. Walter Czapek, who was on duty there, and a few gentlemen from the Filler Group, in order to make a report against unknown persons.

1. of strong suspicion of the desecration of a grave and
2. of strong suspicion of the theft of cultural property.

This was what my attorney Dr. Herbert Eichenseder had advised me to report at this time. And then I opened up and told about Mr. Flatzelsteiner; I mentioned the two people from Burgenland whom he said he had met in the dance-bar "Slovanka Split".

After talks with the leading editors Dichand, Dragon and Haunold as well as with Professors Bankl and Bauer—who were already in the picture—I had become accustomed to causing astonishment with my story. Of course, the police commissioners reacted in the same way. First they shook their heads in doubt, but as I went into more details, they listened to me with more interest. I imagine that the secretary to whom I dictated the three pages of my report had tears in her eyes. Mary Vetsera stolen!—First her unhappy love for the Crown Prince, then her frightful death and now this too.

Hofrat Edelbacher left the room while I was dictating my statement, in order to inform the Vienna Chief of Police, Dr. Gúnther Bögl. Simultaneously, Dr. Czapek informed

1. The office of the State Prosecutor in Vienna and

2. The Institute for Forensic Medicine, whose chief, Georg Bauer, had already been "forewarned" by me.

While the report was being typed, I called the Prior of Heiligenkreuz, who then immediately informed Abbot Gerhard Hradil, the head of the religious establishment, of the "catastrophe." So, I had taken all the steps required by law. First, I had done my duty with respect to the law, and next, I had a noteworthy exclusive story. In this case, besides all my ambition as a journalist, the sequence of events is important.

I also called Mr. Flatzelsteiner in Linz from the Public Safety office. "I have just made my report. Now you must tell the gentlemen from the police where the skeleton is located." I turned the telephone over to Dr. Czapek who took down the name and address of the Roock Transfer Company in Vienna-Meidling.

Two minutes later we were in two cars, led by an operations vehicle with a blue light and siren, on our way to Meidling. It was rush hour, but still we made the rather long trip in twenty-five minutes, avoiding a dozen traffic restrictions. "Why so fast?" I asked the police officer. "In this case, the Public Safety office can neither save a human life nor catch a criminal." Czapek said: "We must act at once. Someone could be there ahead of us and either damage the skeleton—if there really is one—take it away or do something else to it." He said we had to be prepared for any eventuality where a crime is concerned.

No one was there ahead of us. We only met one of the

firm's accountants who was confused by the presence of so many police. A few days before, he had received three closed boxes for storage from Mr. Flatzelsteiner, without any guess of what was in them.

The three crates which were immediately brought forth, enclosed in wrapping paper, contained the coffin cover, the lower part of the coffin and a much smaller metal chest where we found the remains of Mary Vetsera with her clothing, shoes, etc. When the man learned what a strange cargo he was storing, he became quite pale. The police asked him right away what he knew.

He knew nothing.

A half an hour later the forensic doctor Bauer and Szilvássy met us in the courtyard of the transfer and storage company. Szilvássy recognized the metal chest at once, given to him, as containing the great grandmother of Mr. Flatzelsteiner, Theresia Vindona. "The chest is exactly as it was a year ago, when I packed the skeleton into it after my examination."

I was the only one who knew that the skull had been removed for a short time by Mr. Flatzelsteiner, before he placed it on my desk.

While the skeleton was not touched, in order not to cause any damage to it, the coffin and coffin cover were peeled away from the packing. The cardboard was fastened with a yellow adhesive strip from the bedding company "Joka" which was represented by Mr. Flatzelsteiner in Upper Austria. I asked Professor Szilvássy whether the tin coffin might date from the fifties of our century. "Clearly, yes," he said. And that was another indication of the authenticity of the whole affair. After the Second World War, Mary Vetsera's body had been reinterred. This was done, because in April, 1945, Russian soldiers had desecrated the grave, thinking that there might be valuable jewelry in it. The original copper coffin had been so severely damaged that the skeleton had to be placed in a tin coffin on July 7, 1959.

There was another indicator: I had in my hands a photograph of the second interment made in 1959, on which the tin coffin could be recognized. The shape of the coffin was identical with this one. The police asked me to let them have the photograph for purposes of comparison.

Nevertheless, that evening and the next morning I had an uneasy feeling in my stomach. Our headline still read: "Mary Vetsera Stolen from the Grave!" There were many indications that the mortal remains of Crown Prince Rudolf's mistress lay before us. But what proof? For the moment the matter could not be really proven. For myself, I estimated the probability at seventy per cent that this was the genuine Mary Vetsera. Only about thirty per cent spoke against the information I had and according to my feeling. But woe! if the thirty per cent should prove to be true!

I learned the next morning from Dr. Czapek that, on the basis of my report, Mary Vetsera's grave was to be opened immediately. It was December 22nd and there was the problem of finding a stone-mason during the Christmas holidays who would do this work right away. They found one and everything went ahead at once.

I had not expected the authorities to act so quickly. If the grave had been opened three or four months later—normally the mills of the government grind so slowly—then our headlines would probably have been already half forgotten. But in this case: It would have already been seen on the day of our spectacular report on the front page whether Mary Vetsera's body was really there or not!

I could see in my mind's eye the malicious comments of the other newspapers in case Mary were lying peacefully in her grave. Although I had couched the story in relatively cautious terms, I could see in my most daring dreams how the competitors would "carve us up," if our information were false. I do not think that Dichand would have fired me right away, but in that case my professional reputation would have been shot to hell. One of the *Krone* officials said to me on the stairs of the editorial offices: "We should not have done that. I think Vetsera is lying there. Then: Good night!"

The "Good Night!" that we feared might have begun at

noon. By 12:50 P.M. the first of the three heavy gravestones, each weighing about four hundred pounds, was lifted. I was not at Heiligenkreuz myself, as I was again writing a double page for the next day. Three minutes after the raising of the first stone, my colleague Christian Hauenstein, called me on his mobile telephone from the cemetery: "The grave is empty!"

I was relieved of a burden at least as heavy as the stone they had just removed from the grave. The "Hitler Diaries" could remain the journalistic disgrace of the century. My reputation was saved!

Still, one read in the morning edition of a rather wild competitor, which must have gotten its news about Mary Vetsera from the *Krone*, something about a "grotesque story that had just appeared."

At 1 P.M. the midday television news. A live report from the cemetery at Heiligenkreuz. Dozens of reporters, radio and television teams from at home and abroad, forensic doctors, policemen, gendarmes and a frightened Abbot for whom was now confirmed what he must have feared the evening before. "Yes, the grave was not guarded," said Gerhard Hradil in an interview. "The perpetrators were free to remove the coffin."

Every hour I was mentioned in the radio news as the "discoverer" of the affair, and then also on television in the evening. Hans Bankl was a guest on an extended coverage by *Zeit im Bild*. Foreign Minister Alois Mock, who was in Washington at the time with the American President George Bush, had to wait in a Public Broadcasting studio for a channel, until the "Vetsera Report" was finished.

Obviously, there was not yet any thought of its being "finished." Things really started that evening. In Austria and also in many countries of the world. After one-hundred and three years, Mayerling proved to be a theme of unrivaled power.

Flatzelsteiner's Confession
. . . And the Media War

Mary Vetsera interrupted my sleep. The news of her being stolen from the grave went around the world. For days on end in that Christmastime of 1992, I had to be available for television, radio and newspaper colleagues from many countries. They wanted to know everything about Mr. Flatzelsteiner and how I had gotten the story. I looked up a series being planned on the historical background of Mayerling and at night I wrote an article for the next day.

Then on December 26th came the story of the flashlight.

During the three or four personal talks I had with Flatzelsteiner, I always asked him for proof. Proof that the remains in his possession were really those of Mary Vetsera. Once he said to me: "I am certain that it is Mary. One hundred per cent."

"Why are you so certain?"

"Because I looked into it."

"You must explain that more to me, Mr. Flatzelsteiner."

"After I had bought the skeleton, I was naturally not sure if it was in fact that of Vetsera. One evening, I could not bear it any more and went to Heiligenkreuz, to the cemetery, where Mary was buried."

"And—what happened there?"

Flatzelsteiner declared that he had raised the first grave stone with the aid of two automobile jacks and a strong iron bar tied between them and used the gap this made to look into the grave. "And the grave was empty!" To be more exact, the old copper coffin was there (without Mary's skeleton) dating from 1889, on top of which the new tin coffin had been placed in 1959.

It is true that the old coffin remained in the tomb after its desecration by Soviet soldiers and the reinterment that was needed afterwards. Naturally the use of the automobile jacks at the grave seemed strange to me. But what, I ask you, was not strange in this entire story? So, I believed Flatzelsteiner's version more or less (although I could not use it in any way as proof).

Flatzelsteiner said that during his private grave opening the front part of his flashlight fell into the grave. So far, so bad.

A few days after I had made the criminal report, a so-called "Mayerling scholar," as she was called by a newspaper, and her companion, discovered that Vetsera's remains could not have been stolen four years earlier, but between November, 1990, and August, 1991. The "scholar"—she was, by the way, a servant in the press building of the *Kronen Zeitung*—turned out to be such a Vetsera fan that she filmed her grave site every few months with a video camera. Her video soundtrack stated that "in November, 1990, that is, two years after it was robbed, according to Flatzensteiner, the tomb had the same appearance as in past years." But then came August 12, 1991, when the "scholars" could not believe what they saw: The crack between the foremost and middle granite stones, which is usually covered with verdigris, has become wider. The customary traces of weathering have disappeared and the sharp edges of the heavy cover are in splinters, as though someone had used force against it. In addition, there are pieces of freshly broken granite in the fissures! Both of them had the sudden thought that someone had been inside the tomb. They would have reported their observation to the Prior of Heiligenkreuz at that time, but he did not think it was significant. I called Flatzelsteiner. "What do you say to this story?"

"I don't know what to say. I don't feel well, I have back pains and I am nervous." Flatzelsteiner was about to collapse.

I continued. "Could the cracks have occurred at the time you looked into the tomb?"

Flatzelsteiner seized upon the idea gratefully.

"Yes, that is possible."

"When was that?" I asked.

"I don't remember exactly," said the furniture dealer.

"Mr. Flatzelsteiner, think back. It is important. Can the date coincide with that of the video pictures?"

"Yes. It is possible!"

While we were talking, I recalled the story of the flashlight and said to him: "I cannot keep this to myself, for that would make me liable to prosecution. Besides, you ought to discuss the new situation with your attorney."

Flatzelsteiner replied with this memorable statement:

"Unfortunately, that is not possible. He has a bad heart and cannot be excited!"

"Mr. Flatzelsteiner, you should look for a healthy lawyer," I answered, and our "informant," who was by now questionable for many reasons, decided to engage two famous attorneys in Vienna, Adolf and Alfred Kriegler, father and son.

The next day I published the flashlight story in the *Krone*. I must admit that at that moment I still did not think Flatzelsteiner capable of directing this entire affair. I even thought that the flashlight spoke in his favor. It was certain that when he looked into the tomb, he could not retrieve the front part of his flashlight, because he only had a very small crack at his disposal, through which it was impossible to climb. I reflected: If he were the grave robber, he would have had not only a crack, but the whole immense aperture of the grave to use, in order to fetch his flashlight. When the coffin was lifted, two, if not all three, stone slabs had to be removed, and then it would have been easy for him to retrieve his flashlight.

Flatzelsteiner had just left by train on the way to Vienna to meet his new attorneys, the Krieglers, when Dr. Czapek called me from the Public Safety office. He had a request to make of me.

Prior to his first police hearing (two days after my report), the furniture dealer telephoned me. At that time he was under no suspicion and was only referred to by the Public Safety authorities as an "informant." He asked: "Mr. Markus, can I make a statement to the police?"

"Why not?"

"Well, because I have an exclusive contract with your

newspaper."

I wondered later if that was naïveté or was he trying right at the beginning to shield himself from unwelcome questions? Today I presume that the latter was the case; at that time I only laughed.

"Mr. Flatzelsteiner, the exclusive agreement is of course not aimed at the police, but only at other newspapers. You have to speak out."

A good week went by. On December 28th Dr. Czapek called me and asked me again to inform Flatzelsteiner emphatically how the exclusive agreement was to be interpreted. Apparently, whenever he became involved in contradictions, he referred to his contract with us.

I promised Czapek to come Tuesday morning to his Public Safety office, in order to drum into Flatzensteiner the fact that he must answer all questions put to him by the police.

A call to Dr. Kriegler senior. "Tomorrow, eleven o'clock, meeting at the Public Safety office."

The attorney: "From now on we decline to make any statement."

"Yes, but why, for Heaven's sake?"

I did not like that. I had promised Czapek to meet Flatzelsteiner at his office. Besides, the furniture dealer would fall under more suspicion if he refused to make a statement to the police. However, I wanted the whole matter to be clarified and told Dr. Kriegler that I should earnestly request a statement from Flatzelsteiner tomorrow morning (Tuesday).

Late that evening, Kriegler senior telephoned me on behalf of his client.

"We must meet at once. It is very urgent."

It was shortly after 10 P.M. when I entered the "Halali" restaurant at the Neuer Markt in Vienna's inner city. Kriegler and son were already having dinner. Right after my arrival, Kriegler senior surprised me with the words:

"So, it was *him*!"

"Excuse me?"

"Yes, Flatzelsteiner did it himself!"

Now I was just as uncomfortable as I had been a week earlier before the opening of the tomb, when I did not know if Vetsera were lying in it or not. Flatzelsteiner was my informant. How would the other newspapers fall all over me, if it came out that he was the one who had "kidnapped" Mary? Dr. Kriegler tried to cheer me up.

"Tomorrow morning he will tell at the Public Safety office how it really was."

During a long conversation which the attorneys had with their client during the afternoon and evening, it had actually come out that it was Flatzelsteiner himself who did it. Kriegler & Kriegler also gave me the reasons for the upcoming acknowledgment before the police: "Our client never sought money and punishment for robbery would require showing an intention of enrichment. It is our legal opinion that punishment for robbery cannot be sought for that reason alone. And with respect to disturbing the dead, the statute of limitations is already there. Besides, it would have to be investigated by psychiatrists whether Mr. Flatzelsteiner's actions, which are abnormal, do not exclude the possibility of his guilt." Otherwise, a confession would constitute an important basis for mitigation of any penalty. I called Hans Dichand at home and asked him:

"How much time do we still have to change the headline for the morning edition?"

"Till eleven."

I did not want to give him any details, as several people were standing around the telephone in the "Halali." If one mentioned the name "Flatzelsteiner" at that time, it would have attracted attention. All Austria was having "Mayerling fever".

Dichand was standing in front of the building entrance, when I reached the Kaasgraben. My question as to how much time we had to change the front page had made him curious.

"Dichand," I said, my face still pale. "You were right. It was really him. Flatzelsteiner opened the grave himself!"

Now it was essential to act quickly. Dichand took paper and pencil and sketched out the headlines for the morning

edition. "Businessman Admits Desecration of Vetsera Grave."
And then in italics: "Grave Robber's Confession." On page
nine was a report by Dieter Kindermann, who had interviewed
Adolf Kriegler late in the evening about Flatzelsteiner's
confession.

Next morning the news exploded like a bomb. Whereas
all the other newspapers were still speculating who the grave
robber might be, our readers already knew. Of course, this
was not only a struggle for a headline: this time it was more.
We were the ones who had discovered the theft from the grave
and we also had to be the ones who identified the culprit first.
It is needless to ask how the other periodicals would have
reacted if they had gotten to our informant first. Thus, we not
only had an additional lead in reporting, but we were the only
newspaper to have disproven Flatzelsteiner's earlier version.
No serious accusations could be made against us.

Unfortunately, they are not all serious and the competition
fell all over me. The variety paper mentioned before said
"There is much suspicion flowing around the reporter of one
of the dailies, which is celebrating him as a hero." The
magazine *News*, which had refused the story when it was
offered to them by Flatzelsteiner, was more precise. Now it
asserted in a story with illustration, that "Georg Markus . . .
was even under suspicion of having been one of the organizers
of the theft." (In the next edition, the magazine excused itself
for this insinuation for which they could have been sued). The
climax of this campaign came in the television program
"Schwarz auf Weiss," whose anchorman preferred to cross-
examine, rather than interview me.

A little item on the side: Scarcely two months after the
"Mayerling scholar" had caused Flatzelsteiner great trouble
with her video pictures, she invited him to her apartment for
coffee and cake. The two Vetsera fans must have had a great
time in that stimulating atmosphere, surrounded by photographs
of Rudolf and Mary, videotapes of the grave and books on
Mayerling.

A Prince with Many Talents
Life of the Crown Prince

If he had become Emperor, the history of our century might have been quite different. Of course, history does not permit that kind of speculation.

Crown Prince Rudolf was born on August 21, 1858, after two daughters, the ardently-desired Crown Prince of the thirty-eight-year-old Emperor Francis Joseph and his twenty-one-year-old wife Elisabeth, at Laxenburg Castle near Vienna. That was the year when Austria's great general, Count Johann Wenzel Radetzky, died at the age of 91. It was also the year when the fortifications around the Inner City were removed and the Ring Strasse was built. With this step, the Emperor laid the foundation of a modern world capital. The Crown Prince was born into the Vienna of the poets Franz Grillparzer and Johann Nestroy and the painters Hans Makart and Moritz von Schwind.

Five days before Rudolf's birth, the great chandelier in the Schönbrunn Hall of Ceremonies fell from its mooring with a mighty crash. This was taken by the Court to be a bad omen for the future of the youngest Habsburg.

The Crown Prince was to be prepared for his duties as future monarch by draconian punishments. Rudolf's grandmother Sophie appointed a general by the name of Gondrecourt, who was authoritarian and unfeeling, to be responsible for the young Archduke, who undoubtedly suffered permanent psychological injury from the measures his tutor adopted to "harden" him. As early as when he was three years old, he was awakened at night by pistol shots and was drenched with cold water. The youngster had to drill for hours every day. Elisabeth was not permitted to influence the development of the intelligent and sensitive boy in the "Imperial Children's Room" in practically any way.

Finally, it was the "Story of the Wild Hog" which brought about the change. Count Leopold Gondrecourt locked the six-year-old Crown Prince into the Zoological Garden at Lainz and called to him from outside, across the wall: "A wild hog is coming!" The child screamed and ran for his life, until the whole thing turned out to be a joke, which was intended to teach Rudolf toughness and self-preservation.

When the Empress learned of the frightful episode, the cup was full. She said that Gondrecourt's drill would make a dunce of Rudolf and that the "water cures" ordered by the general were just as nonsensical as his other methods of education. Elisabeth went to the Emperor, who hesitated, as he so often did, whether to agree with her or with his mother Sophie, who stood fully behind Gondrecourt.

Then, on August 24, 1865, Elisabeth, who was becoming slowly emancipated, made herself clear in an ultimatum written to Francis Joseph: "I want unconditional power over everything that relates to the children, the choice of their environment, the place of their residence, the entire direction of their education. In a word, I am to be the only one to determine this, until they reach their majority." If the Emperor should not agree to these demands, Elisabeth threatened to leave him forever.

Francis Joseph had no choice. Rudolf received a new tutor in Joseph von Latour, who was decisive in the direction of his life and especially for his liberal outlook. The progressive Latour made the Crown Prince aware of the signs of the new times; inhuman obedience and drill were replaced by understanding and humane warmth. Since this high-minded teacher was responsible for the selection of Rudolf's tutors, there was a favorable change also in the Crown Prince's private instruction.

His history teacher, Joseph Zhisman, introduced the inquisitive boy to the ideas of the Revolution of 1848 and filled him with enthusiasm for democracy and social questions. Whereas Emperor Francis Joseph was convinced of the divine right of his position, there grew in Rudolf a consciousness of his condition that was worldly and progressive.

The ten-year-old was described by his tutor Joseph Latour as follows: "As far as His Imperial Highness' character is concerned, he has a noble heart, much ambition and he does not allow anyone of his age to do better than he does. But he tends towards optimism and tries whenever possible to forget things that are unpleasant. He observes people sharply and his judgment is often appropriate. He is not susceptible to flattery."

It was Latour's only criticism that from time to time Rudolf tended to lie. "This was the only matter that compelled me to correct His Imperial Highness with sharp, severe words." The future heir to the Habsburg Empire showed special talent in the study of foreign languages. Rudolf learned Czech, Hungarian, Polish and French.

Obviously, the best teachers—almost fifty took part in the education of the Crown Prince—could not prevent Rudolf's growing up in complete isolation, without the security of a family circle. Separated from his sisters—Sophie, the firstborn, died two years before his birth; Gisela and Marie Valerie, who was ten years younger, lived in other sections of the gigantic Hofburg and the still larger Schönbrunn Castle—he also had scarcely any contact with his parents. His mother spent most of the year outside the borders of the Monarchy, constantly trying to get away from her husband. Francis Joseph concentrated from early till late pedantically on government business, so that he had neither time nor patience for the problems and needs of his children. In practice, Rudolf only saw his parents on important holidays, official ceremonies, parades and hunts. Austria's Crown Prince grew up almost as an orphan.

It was particularly hard for him that the Emperor prevented him from studying what interested him so much. Besides history and geography, Rudolf was specially interested in natural sciences and loved the world of animals and plants. But in Francis Joseph's thinking, it was not "socially appropriate" for a member of the Imperial House to attend a university.

Thus the Crown Prince, who had been a follower of Charles Darwin since his youth, was forced to seek the knowledge on a private basis which was closed to him on the academic route. He became a friend of the renowned ornithologist and zoologist Alfred Brehm (who dedicated two volumes of his "Brehm's Life of Animals" to the Crown Prince) and accompanied him on trips for scientific research in Hungary and Spain. Rudolf wrote a number of highly-regarded essays and as a twenty-year-old private scholar, published his first book, after having made a scientific expedition, which he entitled "Fifteen Days on the Danube". Recognized by experts as an ornithologist, the Archduke became an honorary member of the Imperial Academy of Sciences and honorary doctor of the universities of Vienna, Budapest and Craców.

Rudolf was also a talented draftsman, but instead of following his inclinations and interests, he was compelled to undergo political and military training, although he knew that he would not be in a position to use his "professional education" to be monarch in the foreseeable future. Francis Joseph was in the best of health and was not thinking of abdicating the throne in favor of his son.

Although the sensitive young man was not attracted to the military career, he took the duties given him as officer very seriously. They were also the only ones entrusted to him by his father. Rudolf was appointed colonel of the 19th Infantry Regiment when he was two days old and climbed the career ladder very quickly, which was due only to his family origin.

At twenty-two, he was a brigadier general and commanding officer of a regiment in Prague; at twenty-four, he was a lieutenant field marshal. During his five years at the Hradčany Castle, Rudolf attempted a rapprochement with the Czech nationalists. From 1883 on, he was assigned to the capital, where he referred to his regiment as his real "home." All his life he clung to the army, which was for him the last bastion of the Double Monarchy. As a soldier, he also took an interest in social matters, proposed an increase in officers' pay and improvement of the soldiers' mess.

Nevertheless, his attachment to the army went so far that he quarreled in 1883 with Archduke Johann Salvator, who later left the Imperial House as Johann Orth and renounced all his privileges. This attracted a great deal of attention. During a lecture at the Officers' Club in Vienna, his cousin took a stand against the continuation of the strict training methods in the Army, saying, "We do not drill, we educate." The Crown Prince answered in a conservative and intentionally provocative way: "We drill *and* educate!"

Rudolf hated the strict life of the Court just as his mother did, and alongside his military career developed many ideas for changing the political, economic and social situation of the Monarchy and hastening the advancement of technology and science. Although he rejected the idea of Socialism, he leaned towards the "left," as that term might apply to conditions at that time. He admired the French Revolution whose ideas and principles, he thought, had lifted the nations of Europe from the grisly guillotine and had rejuvenated, strengthened and ennobled them. Rudolf supported a shortening of the working day and prohibition of child labor. From his teacher Carl Menger, the founder of the Austrian School of National Economy, he learned to combine economic postulates with social interests. "It was discernible from his questions and comments," Professor Menger said later, "that even as a young man, Rudolf was conscious of his high calling."

This was one of many demands made by the young Rudolf, which was decades too early for the history of the world: "The institution of property also has its undeniable dark side; one of its greatest evils is the stark distinction between poor and rich which has come about in the course of time. So, from an ideal standpoint, we must consider a rather equally divided wealth and prosperity for all as a source of moral progress."

It was Rudolf's tragedy that he was never able to realize his ideas, being condemned to endless waiting. He had to watch from the sidelines as national separatism constantly increased in the Monarchy and there was more agitation, whereas he was forced out of politics. Maladjusted and free-thinking like Empress Elisabeth, even revolutionary in many ways, the Crown Prince became an outsider at the Viennese Court.

Like his mother, he considered the throne an antiquated institution and among his friends he even thought of himself as a future "President of a Republic." He was not opposed to the Monarchy. On the contrary, he wanted to preserve his father's inheritance with all his power, but he did not give it much realistic chance for the future. Emulating his model, Joseph II, Rudolf felt much closer to the growing liberal bourgeoisie than to the aristocracy, which bored him stiff, or even the clergy, which was extremely powerful at that time.

"The kingdom stands there as a powerful ruin," he said in notes he left behind. "It will remain from now until tomorrow, but will finally decline. It has lasted for centuries and it was good as long as the nation allowed itself to be led blindly, but now its mission has come to an end; all people are free and this ruin will fall in the next storm." These were not the only prophetic words of the Crown Prince.

We do not know if Rudolf would have become a great statesman or whether he could have saved Austria-Hungary. We can only presume that he would not have made the same mistakes, at least in that way. But as long as he lived, he saw no chance for changing, improving or doing anything. He was not the only one chosen for the rôle with which it is scarcely humanly possible to cope: that of having to wait, as Crown Prince, for his own father's (or mother's) death. There are several cases like that in history, although they turned out differently. The Habsburg Joseph I had to wait a relatively long time before his father, Emperor Leopold I, died in 1705, after having ruled for nearly fifty years. Joseph had only six years himself to rule before being carried away by an epidemic of smallpox. The ninety-year-old German Emperor Wilhelm I was succeeded by his son Friedrich III, who succumbed to cancer of the larynx after ruling for only ninety-nine days. England's Edward VII was sixty when he finally came to power. His mother, Queen Victoria, was eighty-one and had ruled for sixty-three years. After Rudolf, Archduke Francis Ferdinand also had to experience the tragedy of being Crown Prince, until his assassination at Sarajevo. And more recently it is England's Prince Charles whom fate has forced to wait for decades. Decades devoted to preparation for the office of sovereign, without being given significant duties.

Crown Prince Rudolf felt that he was useless. His attempts to convince his father of his own progressive ideas failed when met by the Emperor's inflexibility. The latter excluded Rudolf from all government business. The Crown Prince—like all other subjects—was not even permitted to ask the Emperor a question or speak about any certain matter.

The conflict between the two first men in the Empire was programmed in advance. Rudolf wrote in a letter to his former tutor Latour about his father: "Our Emperor has no friend. His character and his nature do not allow it. He stands isolated on his pinnacle; he talks to his servants on matters affecting the work of each individual, but he scrupulously avoids conversation. For this reason he knows so little of how people think and feel, of the outlook and opinions of the nation. The only thing he reads in the newspapers are the sections marked in red."

When there was conversation on rare occasions between Rudolf and the Emperor, Francis Joseph did not even try to understand the ambitiously presented views of his son, but scornfully dismissed them with the words: "Rudolf is talking nonsense again."

Since "talking nonsense" with his father, whom he respected because of his authority, but whom he was never able to approach in a human or political relationship, seemed to be pointless, Rudolf sought contact with circles that were quite different. He joined liberal groups, showed benevolent interest in the world of the Freemasons, fraternized with coachmen and Heurigen singers, wrote anonymous articles for his friend Moriz Szeps' *Neue Wiener Tagblatt*, often criticizing the government of Prime Minister Count Eduard Taaffe, one of the closest advisors of his father.

Moriz Szeps, who came from a distinguished Jewish family, was one of the most outstanding newspapermen of his time. In 1881, he met the Crown Prince through Carl Menger and was able to get him as an author for his widely read and influential paper. The collaboration was profitable for both:

Rudolf supplied the editor-in-chief and publisher with news from the Court; Moriz Szeps, who was related to Georges Clemenceau through the marriage of his daughter Sophie, provided the Crown Prince, who was entirely isolated from political affairs by his father, with news from France and other countries.

Rudolf, whose yearning for a father-figure had remained unfulfilled till then, found a fatherly friend in Moriz Szeps, who was twenty-four years older, whom, in contrast with Francis Joseph, he could openly admire and with whom he felt "related through a community of ideas and outlook."

After a little more than a year, the cooperation of the Crown Prince with the extreme liberal journalist, which seemed odd to many people, blew up and caused a gigantic scandal at Court. The conservative Archduke Albrecht informed the Emperor, whereupon Rudolf was placed under surveillance around the clock and was severely restricted even in his private activities from then on.

The principal political opponents of the Crown Prince and his journalistic friends were the German Nationalists, led by the Reichsrat Deputy Georg Ritter von Schönerer. With their all-German national ideology, they favored dissolution of the monarchy, to be followed by absorption of the German-speaking parts into the German Empire. It was mostly anti-Semites and nationalists who opposed Szeps' newspaper. The hatred of the militant extremists went so far, that, on March 8, 1888, Schönerer broke into the editorial rooms of the *Tagblatt* and physically attacked several journalists, who had reported the death of the German Emperor Wilhelm I. too soon. For this, Schönerer was sentenced to four months in prison, lost his right to vote for five years, lost his seat in the Reichsrat, his title of nobility and his rank as a Reserve officer.

Yet, on order of Prime Minister Taaffe, the *Tagblatt* was also temporarily closed.

Of course these police measures only strengthened Rudolf's political convictions of liberalism and humanism. The Crown Prince was aware of the fateful development of demagogical racial hatred more than any of his contemporaries. In this he agreed with his father, who wrote to Elisabeth following the rioting after the election of Karl Lueger as mayor of Vienna: "Anti-Semitism is a sickness that reaches remarkably right to the highest levels . . . its abuses are frightful."

In foreign affairs, Rudolf sailed in a direction diametrically opposite the official policy. Whereas the Emperor and Taaffe clung firmly to their alliance with the German Empire, Rudolf in commentaries and leading articles favored a rapprochement with England and France. The Crown Prince saw in both the domestic and foreign policies of the government possible causes of the collapse of the Habsburg Empire which seemed irresistible. In a short memorandum on the problems in the Balkans, the Crown Prince showed real clairvoyance when he warned that an anti-Austrian government might come to power in Belgrade which could cause difficulties for the Monarchy in the occupied provinces of Bosnia and Herzegovina. "This situation, being intolerable, will force us to act. An invasion of Serbia would be a cause for war with Russia, which we should start against a completely anti-Austrian Balkan peninsula from the Black Sea to the Adriatic. Not only the present would be at stake, but the whole future, for which we are responsible to the coming generations."

His activity as journalist and writer was not limited to the field of politics. Besides the ornithological publications already mentioned and several travel books (*A Trip to the Orient*, published in 1881 in two volumes, attracted much attention and was translated into English and Italian), he also wrote essays on hunting which he loved above everything, and wrote an anonymous critical pamphlet on spiritualism. Together with his tutor Carl Menger, who referred to him as an excellent writer of cultural essays, Rudolf published his famous pamphlet *Austrian Nobility* in 1878 at Munich, in which he declared that the nobles had no right to "devote themselves exclusively to enjoying life." He said that instead of that, the aristocrats had a "duty deriving from their social station to carry out the governmental responsibilities entrusted to them as men, but as adolescents to prepare for them. As long as a feeling for this duty is not present in the Austrian nobility and in every member of it, as long as it is not felt to be an honor to accept that duty and a disgrace to avoid it, one cannot anticipate improvement in the present conditions of our nobility and its present position is greatly endangered." Here we see the contradiction in Rudolf's life, as so often before. For he in no way went down in history as a model for the fulfillment of duty, in particular as one of the highest representatives of the nobility.

Rudolf's most significant publication was the monumental edition of *The Austro-Hungarian Monarchy in Word and Picture*, which appeared in twenty-four volumes. As sponsor of the work and author of numerous articles in it, he presented in this, together with well-known artists and scientists, a comprehensive overview of the Crownlands, which he heartily embraced. Among the 430 persons who collaborated in this Crown Prince edition were prominent contemporaries like Carl Menger, Anton Gindely, Emil Zuckerkandl, Eduard Hanslick and Peter Rosegger. The books became quite popular. The authors wrote on a high level on altogether 12,000 pages about the historical, economic and cultural characteristics and the particular lifestyle of the population and the variety of the nationalities. The final volumes, in German and Hungarian, were not printed till after Rudolf's death. The first was solemnly presented to the Emperor, who had supported the whole project in its idea and financially, on December 1, 1885.

Maurus Jokai, the Hungarian editor of the work, described the reception by the Emperor at the Hofburg. "It will always remain for me an unforgettable scene. The King's son before his father, the crowned ruler of the Austro-Hungarian Monarchy, as a writer, presenting the first product of his literary work to the overall sovereign like a trophy! And the ruler's face spontaneously reflected the joy in a father's heart. He gave his son an encouraging answer, urged him to persevere and expressed his satisfaction. Then he turned to me and asked: 'Did my son actually write that Introduction?'"

The scene was typical of the relationship between Francis Joseph and Rudolf. On one hand, it displayed a certain paternal pride, but on the other, the Emperor was unable to give Rudolf credit for any accomplishment.

Meanwhile, the father-son conflict continued. The two men were too different. Francis Joseph, the conservative, entire first servant of the country, who seemed to have lost in the execution of his duties any human warmth. And Rudolf, the progressive-thinking intellectual, of whom the great surgeon Theodor Billroth wrote on the day of his death: "Among those who knew him, there can be no doubt of the Crown Prince's high intelligence. His was a nature similar to that of Joseph II and Max of Mexico."

For many people, Rudolf would have been the right ruler for the twentieth century. Mayerling put an end to that dream.

I said at the beginning of this chapter that history does not allow speculation, but let us try it anyway. Without Mayerling, Rudolf could have meant: A century without war, for with Rudolf there would have been no Francis Ferdinand, without him no Sarajevo, and without Sarajevo, no First World War. And without the First, probably not the Second either. It is agreed that this is a very daring speculation, but we can still dream.

After all, the real greatness of the unfortunate Rudolf were his dreams of a better world.

A Suggestion from the Capuchin Crypt
"Operation Hamlet"
and the Mayerling Syndrome

One day after his confession to his attorney, Helmut Flatzelsteiner made an official statement at a hearing before members of the Vienna Public Safety Office, in the presence of Dr. Kriegler junior, as to how the robbery of the grave at Heiligenkreuz had occurred. He revealed the details of the police report to my colleague, Dieter Kindermann.

"Why have you lied until now?" Kindermann asked him in the office of his attorneys.

"I was afraid," said Flatzelsteiner.

"Afraid of what?"

"A person who is afraid does not need a motive," he answered shortly. Then, with his hands in the air, he explained how he had come to this fateful idea. "I bought all the books I could about the death of Archduke Rudolf and his mistress and was possessed with the thought of lifting the veil from this secret. I also suffered from psychic problems after my wife's death."

"But Mr. Flatzelsteiner, that does not excuse the desecration of a grave," said Kindermann.

"I was not interested in the remains, but in the historical truth: How did Mary die? From a shot in the head, poison, a stab wound or abortion. I took pictures of the grave at Heiligenkreuz and measured it, in order to know many automobile jacks, bars and plates I should need for opening the grave."

Somewhat later, on January 31, 1993, Flatzelsteiner said during an interview on the German "Spiegel TV" that he had found the decisive statement in a book by the physician Gerd Holler, where he wrote on page 360 "that the key to the secret of Mayerling can only lie in the mortal remains of Mary Vetsera." When he read that, Flatzelsteiner knew that it was his mission to act.

55

The furniture dealer insists that he did indeed meet two men from Burgenland in 1988 at a discotheque in Budejovice (Budweis) and told them of his fantastic plan. On another occasion, he declared that they were two of his acquaintances whose names he would not give. "It was not till three years later that I took courage to execute my plan, when the two came to visit me in Linz. They asked me if I dared to do it, whereupon I answered: 'Will you go along?'"

In the evening of that same day—it was probably July 8, 1991—Flatzelsteiner drove with his accomplices in a blue Ford Transit-Bus to Heiligenkreuz. In the vehicle they had packed four automobile jacks, iron bars, plates and wood, "so that no blade of grass would be crushed on the tomb". The opening of the grave occurred at about 10 P.M. and went forward without difficulty, as Flatzelsteiner had planned it for years like a General Staff officer.

When the coffin lay before him in the darkness, Flatzelsteiner greeted the body of Crown Prince Rudolf's mistress, as he told us later, in English, saying: "Dear Mary, we'll have a good time!"

Flatzelsteiner returned home with his strange "booty" during the early morning hours of the next day. He threw a blanket over the stolen coffin and slid it onto a bench in his cellar at Linz.

"The next day I racked my brains as to how I could open the coffin, which was soldered shut." So he described what was probably the most macabre part of his adventure. "I telephoned a skilled worker at the Capuchin Crypt in Vienna for advice. He said: 'We always pry the tin caskets open.'"

The furniture dealer was "very disappointed" when he had finally opened the coffin with a pulley. "I had anticipated something pretty, but it was all wet, dirty and smelled awful. I set about cleaning the skeleton, just as though an anthropologist were looking over my shoulder. I laid the mortal remains on metal sheets in a shady place in my garden to dry,"

The amateur scientist set about unraveling the secret of Mayerling in his own way. He said: "I sorted the entirely disarranged bones according to the information in a book on anatomy." Then he took photographs (which were given me later). Afterwards, he called in the medical experts, telling them the made-up story of the skeleton of his great grandmother.

I spoke again with Helmut Flatzelsteiner on the telephone a few days after his confession. For the first time, I was talking to him with the knowledge that he was not merely the purchaser of the skeleton, as he always said, but the perpetrator of the robbery. On one hand, by his escapade he had brought me the story of my life, but on the other, into great difficulties. Several media were now suggesting that I had thought he was an "informant," but not the culprit. In such cases I always said that it was not my duty to convict him, but that of the police.

Now I asked Flatzelsteiner if it had been easy to find physicians to examine the skeleton of his "great-grandmother" Theresia Vindona without a detailed statement. In reality there had been no problems on that subject, according to Flatzelsteiner. Only Dr. Heinrich of the Histological Institute of the University of Vienna asked for proof that he was in fact related to Theresia Vindona. Thereupon Flatzelsteiner drew a family tree of his own family where he simply inserted the name Theresia Vindona as that of his great-grandmother. A small absurdity occurred to Dr. Heinrich about it: According to Flatzelsteiner's geneological tree, Theresia Vindona, the great-grandmother, had no children!

Nevertheless, the doctor sent him with his "childless great-grandmother" to Professor Szilvássy of the Institute for Forensic Medicine. I asked him in the course of my later research if anyone with a skeleton could come to have it examined. This was Szilvássy's answer:

"At the Institute for Forensic Medicine we receive one-hundred to one-hundred and fifty corpses or skeletons per year for identification (determination of age, sex, duration of interment, etc.). Most of these are based on a request from the Public Prosecutor to determine the cause of death. In addition, skeletons are also brought to us by private persons, having been discovered during excavation, in the forest or by house or street construction. After forty years in the ground, there is no prosecution and therefore no requirement for reporting." And that was the case of "Theresia Vindona," who died one-hundred years ago.

Flatzelsteiner's defender, Dr. Kriegler, said after the hearing: "My client only wanted to help bring out the historical truth about the death of Mary Vetsera. It could turn out by psychiatric examination that he is suffering from an illness which I want to call 'Mayerling syndrome.'"

"The crime of the century" was described in the next edition of *Profile* by Klaus Kamolz and Alfred Worm under the title of "Operation Hamlet" (after the Danish prince Hamlet, who received the skull of the royal jester Yorick from two grave diggers). They defined the "Mayerling Syndrome" discovered by Dr. Kriegler as "a transformation of the thought processes which is not yet current in medical language, separating yesterday from today, and having as symptom an irrepressible urge to solve the Mayerling puzzle."

Of Midwives and the Powers of Darkness
Two Versions: Abortion and Murder

After more than one hundred years, the Linz furniture dealer, Helmut Flatzelsteiner, was driven by the desire to achieve what historians, medical men and other scientists could not: to bring light to the tragedy of the Crown Prince and finally "solve" the mystery of Mayerling.

The mystery of Mayerling. How could it come to the point where the death of a couple of young lovers could still so deeply affect so many people more than a hundred years after the event? The answer, as we see it now: It was the tactics of the Court of wanting to keep everything secret, which worked in precisely the opposite direction. If a commission had tried to clarify in 1889 what had taken place in the Crown Prince's hunting lodge; if it had been revealed at once that there was not one corpse, but two, then the Mayerling legend would not have continued for so long, at least in that form.

But as it was, the door was opened wide to speculation. And nothing in that has changed in a hundred years. Dozens of versions of the story are still circulating, all claiming to "prove" the "real cause" of Rudolf's and Mary's death. During the days and weeks of the reports of the desecration of tne grave in Heiligenkreuz, countless "witnesses" wrote and called me. Their grandfather or great-grandfather had been a hunter at the Court, a chamberlain, a coachman to the Royal family or were relatives or friends of the Crown Prince, and everyone had his version of the drama ready: murder, suicide, sequelae of an abortion, killed with a champagne bottle, poisoned, hunting accident, a jealous lovers' quarrel, victims of a political assassination . . . there were and still are no limits to fantasy.

But besides the version of a double suicide, which are the possible interpretations of the tragedy that can be taken with relative seriousness? In past years there have been two hypotheses that caused a great deal of sensation: (1) Mary's death after an abortion, and then the suicide of the Crown Prince, and (2) an "assassination plot by foreign powers."

The physician and Mayerling scholar Gerd Holler put forward the abortion theory for the first time in his book on Mayerling in 1980. These were the circumstances he gave as evidence:

Immediately after the Mayerling drama, Count Constantin Nigra, the Italian ambassador in Vienna, reported to his government at Rome: "A girl was found beside the Crown Prince at Mayerling, the daughter of Baroness Vetsera, who said that she was pregnant or thought she was" (reported by the *Corriere della Sera* on June 13, 1907).

Rudolf himself told Countess Larisch "that the affair with Mary was not without guilt" (quoted from the memoirs of Marie Larisch).

Princess Julie Odescalchi-Zichy asserted that Mary "was four months pregnant (*Wiener Morgenpost*, October 10, 1927).

On February 5, 1889, the police informant Milarow (real name: Dr. Florian Meissner) reported to the Chief of Police, Baron Krauss, that the "four-month pregnancy of a Baroness Wecera (?), who is considered an ideal beauty" may be involved in the Mayerling affair.

A certain Emil Miller asserted that his grandmother, the midwife Theresia Miller, was engaged by Countess Larisch to go to England with Mary Vetsera for delivery of a child. In 1978, Dr. Holler spoke with Emil Miller's widow, who confirmed that statement by her husband.

Another witness adduced by Holler was Countess Zoe Wassilko-Serecki, who stated that in 1919, at the castle of her uncle, the Austrian Imperial Prime Minister Count Eduard Taaffe, at Ellischau in Bohemia, she read the Mayerling papers, "twenty to thirty pages marked 'streng reservat' (very secret)." She gathered from the secret memorandum that "Vetsera was expecting, in the third or fourth month, I do not recall exactly, but it was certain that she was, as expressed therein." (Document in the Austrian State Archives, Vienna, 1955.)

What did the doctor conclude on the basis of this evidence

and the statements of these witnesses? "I am convinced that Mary Vetsera was pregnant and this is no longer questioned by historians." And then he came to the two dates which are specially emphasized in Mary's diary: November 5, 1888, and January 13, 1889. "For a long time, these entries were interpreted to mean that Mary was with Rudolf for the first time in the Hofburg on November 5th and that they first had intimate contact on January 13th. As a physician, I see it with different eyes: November 5, 1888, first intimate contact; January 13, 1889, complete confirmation of pregnancy."

So Gerd Holler interprets Mary's letter to her piano teacher Hermine Tobis ("We both lost our heads. Now we belong to each other in body and soul") as follows: "In January, Rudolf and Mary had to decide whether the pregnancy was to be carried to term or interrupted."

Of course, "problems" of that kind occurred frequently in the Imperial household. They were almost always solved in a "discreet" manner. A public official or officer was compelled to marry the woman in question, for which he was promised an extraordinary career. In Mary's case such a solution was not possible, since she was engaged to Miguel of Braganza, a member of the royal family of Portugal. Dr. Holler said: "Heinrich Baltazzi-Scharschmied, Mary's cousin, told me that the two were engaged to be married."

Therefore, the only way Mary could protect her future was to have an abortion. The doctor said "there is no doubt that the midwife Theresia Miller, residing at Wien I, Himmelpfortgasse, performed that operation." And this is how it was done, according to him: "On Monday, January 28, 1889, Countess Larisch brought Mary, with Rudolf's personal coachman Bratfisch, to the Hofburg. There the Crown Prince disappeared with Mary and reappeared a half hour later without her."

During that time, Dr. Holler asserted that a surgical operation took place in the Crown Prince's rooms, using a catheter which was to remain in the uterus for 24 hours. And in fact, on January 29th—Mary and Rudolf were already at

Mayerling—the Court telegrapher Julius Schuldes stated that "a woman appeared, who left a quarter of an hour later." It is Gerd Holler's theory that "when another midwife removed the catheter, there occurred a hemorrhage that could not be arrested and Mary died as a result."

A few hours after Mary's death, Rudolf went "calmly to meet Death, which alone can save my good name" (from Rudolf's farewell letter to Stephanie).

Further evidence was given in the description of Rudolf's corpse by the Court secretary, Dr. Heinrich Slatin: "His face was scarcely disfigured, but the top of the skull was blown off. There was blood and brain fragments were flowing out, as it seemed to me, from a gunshot at a relatively short distance. Beside him was the body of a beautiful young woman."

The conclusion: "If Mary had been shot, she would have looked exactly the same as Rudolf. "But she was unharmed from outside."

The historian Brigitte Hamann does not accept the theory of an unsuccessful abortion: "According to Holler, Rudolf's death was the sudden decision of a healthy young man who was in complete harmony with himself and the world. For Holler, there were no antecedents to this death other than the love affair with the seventeen-year-old Mary, about which he can tell us nothing new."

The second hypothesis, which became quite "popular" in past years, comes from Austria's last Empress, Zita, who confided to my colleague Dieter Kindermann that she was convinced that Crown Prince Rudolf became the victim of a political assassination plot.

This revelation started with former Federal Chancellor Bruno Kreisky, who told Kindermann in May, 1982, that the former Empress would like to come to Austria "to die," as he expressed it. At that time, the widow of the Emperor still had to live in exile in Switzerland, because, since 1918, she had refused to sign a statement relinquishing her rights as former Empress.

Kreisky sought, and found, "a humane solution" and in

so doing suggested: "Ask Zita right away, what really happened at Mayerling."

Shortly thereafter, Kindermann was sitting in front of the 90-year-old former Empress at the Johannisstift Zizers in the canton of Graubünden. And Zita revealed: "Crown Prince Rudolf did not commit suicide; he became the victim of a political assassination plot." She named five members of the Habsburg family as witnesses to her theory: Emperor Francis Joseph, his daughters Gisela and Marie Valerie, his sister-in-law Maria Theresia and Marie José, the wife of the Duke in Bavaria. She said that those witnesses had confided to her under the seal of silence, that Rudolf was the victim of an international ccnspiracy.

Zita: "When Emperor Francis Joseph was asked why the House of Habsburg had never done anything to erase the stain that the Crown Prince should go down in history as a murderer and suicide, he answered: 'At that time I could not act in any other way. The monarchy was at stake. The truth would have shaken the foundations of the Empire. Everything will be published after my death. Then the poor Rudolf will be entirely rehabilitated."

According to Zita, Francis Joseph asked her husband, as soon as he became Emperor, to open a certain drawer in his writing desk, where all the papers about Mayerling lay. To this she said: "After the Emperor's funeral, when Charles and I went to look at Schönbrunn Castle, there was only a pile of empty sheets of paper in that folder."

Zita spoke about the background of the assassination plot that she alleged: "There was an international conspiracy to drive Emperor Francis Joseph from the throne. People tried to draw the Crown Prince into the conspiracy, because his critical attitude towards the Court camarilla and the militant ally, Emperor Wilhelm II, was well known. Crown Prince Rudolf indignantly rejected this approach, saying: Yes, there is a lot to criticize, but everything has its limits. I shall not go along with this. I am a loyal son of the Emperor. I shall relentlessly expose this conspiracy.'"

Archduke Karl Ludwig, one of the Emperor's brothers, warned Rudolf not to inform his father of this atrocious plan. "If you make it public, they will kill you!"

It was Zita's theory that the conspirators had anticipated Rudolf's revelation of the plot by the double murder at Mayerling.

Although Dieter Kindermann's interview in 1983 resulted in headlines throughout the world, historians accused the former Empress of advocating this theory only for the purpose of eliminating the stain of murder and suicide from the Habsburg family during her husband's beatification process. But Zita held fast to it in many conversations, even before witnesses: "It was an assassination plot!"

A few months after that interview, the author Erich Feigl known as loyal to the Empire (kaisertreu), published a chapter on Mayerling in his book on Emperor Charles, which names two persons as organizers of the assassination plot: France's later Prime Minister Georges Clemenceau, as its political leader, and a Grand Officer of the Legion of Honor, Cornelius Herz, as leader of the execution commando.

It was said that behind the plot lay the desire of the French to win over Austria-Hungary as an ally against the German Empire. Whereas they saw a possible partner in Rudolf, they knew that Francis Joseph would never break his alliance with Emperor Wilhelm.

The historian, Adam Wandruszka, wrote as follows about Zita's version of Mayerling:

"This theory of murder, in contradiction to all of the facts that have been proven for decades, contains nothing new and not a shadow of proof; instead, it reechoes the rumors which were current before 1918 . . . Rudolf's farewell letters, published since 1935, of undoubted authenticity, are not 'depressive letters,' but relatively short announcements of suicide . . . . The farewell letters of Baroness Vetsera, which have likewise become known, supplement and emphasize Rudolf's farewell letters and thereby the irrevocable fact of suicide. It is noteworthy that Empress Zita does not mention in a single word the Baroness, who played a decisive role in the final hours before the joint death which she had desired."

Zita's version of the death was not the only one that saw the Crown Prince's death as the result of a political assassination. The writer Alexander Lernet-Holenia even declared that there were members of the Imperial family behind Rudolf's death. According to him, the Crown Prince had organized a coup d'état against his father, whereupon the Archdukes Karl Ludwig, Albrecht and Wilhelm dispatched two officers to Mayerling. There was a struggle, during which a shot was fired.

In December, 1992, when the grave robbery became known, Zita's eldest son, Otto von Habsburg, cast doubt on his mother's statement during an ORF interview with Nora Frey. He said: "I believe most in the version of a double suicide. As long as I live, the secret of Mayerling will not be completely resolved."

"He Must Die Because He Has Killed"
An Indirect Look into Otto's Strongbox

A few days after Otto von Habsburg's radio interview we learned why he said that the secret of Mayerling would not be completely resolved as long as he lived. On January 2, 1993, an article appeared in the daily newspaper *Der Standard* by Marie-Thérèse Hartig in which the thirty-year-old journalist of aristocratic origin wrote that her ninety-one-year-old great-uncle Kurt Paümann, who was living in Canada, had given a strongbox to Otto von Habsburg in 1985 that contained sensational documentary material about the Mayerling case. There were also the crime weapon—Rudolf's army revolver with ammunition—handwritten farewell letters, a lock of hair from each of the dead persons, and a handkerchief. She said that Paümann had inherited the box from his father, Freiherr Eduard Paümann, who had been a member of Emperor Charles's staff as a privy councillor. The legend ran in the family that in the hectic days between the abdication of the last Emperor and the proclamation of the Republic said box, with the crime weapon, which had officially disappeared, was given to the Freiherr "for safekeeping."

Over the century, the box went "traveling": Kurt Paümann, the son, was married to a Jewess, whom he accompanied to Canada in 1938, as they fled from the Nazis. In their hand-luggage was the box, eight by five inches in size, padded and covered with cloth! It remained in Paümann's possession until the mid-eighties. Then the old immigrant gave the important evidence to his daughter who immediately informed Otto von Habsburg. The transfer of the carefully-preserved strongbox took place at a bank in Hamburg in 1985. The Emperor's son did not seem surprised at the contents of the box, according to those present at the time. Otto told his family that when he received the first call and heard the name Paümann, he was able to imagine what had been kept so long in that box. Until the publication of the matter by the newspaperwoman Marie-

Thérèse Hartig, Otto von Habsburg had never mentioned the box in public, although he had received the evidence eight years before.

Now I questioned the Emperor's son about the mysterious box. "Yes," Habsburg confirmed, "some documents relative to the death of the Crown Prince were in fact given to me."

"Is the revolver with which Crown Prince Rudolf shot himself in the parcel you received?"

Habsburg: "In this matter, I should not like to speak about details."

"Where are the articles today?"

"Look, I deal a great deal with history, but only when it brings us ahead. The history of the Balkans is important at this time, but not that of Mayerling. Therefore I am not personally interested in the subject. I have given the entire bundle of papers to a member of my family, who is more interested in them."

"Would you give me his name?"

"Please understand that I should not like to do that."

Thus the Habsburgs are continuing along the way which has led for more than a hundred years to the regular dissemination of frequently hair-raising speculations. If Otto had "put the cards on the table," the Mayerling debate would not be silenced, but it would still slowly calm down. However, in this manner new theories will continue to arise every few years.

There would conceivably not have been a self-appointed "Mayerling buff" named Flatzelsteiner, if the Habsburg family were ready to contribute to clarification of the mystery.

Shortly after the publication of my Habsburg interview, Austrian Television showed a documentary program on Mayerling which took the historical facts into account as well as what had been learned about the grave robbery up to then. Malte Olschewski, the organizer, brought serious accusations in the program against the present-day members of the Habsburg family: "They give no answer to questions about Mayerling. Otto has come into possession of important pieces of evidence, beyond loyalty to the Crown. He is not willing to make them public . . . In the name of Rudolf's direct descendants, one has to ask: Where does Otto get the right to locked boxes and unknown documents? Otto is only distantly related to Rudolf. His great-grandfather Karl Ludwig was a brother of Francis Joseph. Otto's position as head of the family derives from the two-year rule of his father. The refusal to contribute to Mayerling should not strengthen that position."[2]

In fact, one ought to expect that individuals capable of contributing to the solution of this unique crime in world history, if no longer for legal reasons, still for moral and historical ones, would do everything to bring it about. But the House of Habsburg remains silent, still after a hundred years. This is undoubtedly because the Mayerling story is the most embarrassing in the century-long history of the dynasty. The family should take the position that the great interest the people still demonstrate would subside as soon as one "allowed the dead to rest" (Otto von Habsburg). But in 1993 they are making the same mistake as in 1889. Remaining silent allows the myth to survive, for it is only by withholding present evidence that new, fantastic versions can be generated.

This does nothing good for Rudolf's memory. The constantly recurring speculations about Mayerling conceal, from a historical point of view, the positive sides of the Crown Prince's personality. Rudolf's life and work could be sooner appreciated, once his death is completely understood. In this, the head of the family, Otto von Habsburg—in contrast to his mother, who clung to the theory of an assassination plot till her death in 1989—has a very realistic view of the whole story. And he is one of the few persons in the world who knows about that box and the evidence it contains.

Nevertheless, Otto von Habsburg was to permit me a small, indirect view of the contents of that box. During our interview,

---

[2] Quoted from the television program "Mayerling: Myths without End" by Malte Olschewski, January 28, 1993, ORF2.

when he told me emphatically that the strongbox would continue to be locked, I asked him this question: "Which of the many Mayerling versions might be confirmed by the documents?"

Otto's reply was short and to the point. "The documents clearly confirm the theory presented by Emil Franzel in his book on Mayerling."

Whereupon I immediately obtained a copy of the book by that author, since deceased, entitled *Kronprinzen Mythos und Mayerling-Legenden*, which had appeared in 1963 and had long been out of print. Even if we cannot see the strongbox, I thought, we should at least discover how the act can be construed on the basis of its contents. Franzel wrote: "The Emperor himself determined that his people had a right to truth and ordered that the first version (Note: 'heart attack') be corrected. That horrible thing, suicide, was admitted. Rumor then drew the conclusion that if the strictly Catholic Court declared suicide as the cause of death, what must really have happened? What horrible crimes had to be hushed up, if it was thought necessary to pretend there had been a suicide? Soon it was being said that no matter what the rumors, the truth was still more frightful, and finally, when soon it was known, in spite of all attempts at concealment and measures of security, that a female body had been discovered in the community of Alland, that of a certain Baroness Vetsera, buried at Heiligenkreuz, an avalanche of rumors was produced that is still rumbling on today."[3]

Of all the "rumors," the worst by far was this: The Crown Prince did not only lay a hand upon himself, but also took a young, innocent girl with him to death. "With him to death" was a euphemistic way of saying: He shot her!

Emil Franzel on Baroness Vetsera's death: "When the ecstatic girl declared, without apparent hesitation, that she was

---

[3] Alland is a village 8 mi. WNW of Baden in Lower Austria.

ready to die with Rudolf, he must have lost his self-control entirely. It is reported that there was a violent discussion between him and the Emperor on January 26th, but there were no witnesses to it. Reports of the tone and subject of that fateful conversation are based on conjecture. Still, it can be inferred from following events and Rudolf's last statements that the Emperor may have ordered him to give up his previous lifestyle or his adventure with Vetsera. That Rudolf had neither the courage nor the strength to keep his word; that he could no longer withdraw from what he had promised the girl— whether marriage or mutual death—and preferred to break the word he had given the Emperor, this is the most probable *point d'honneur* that concerned the doomed man in his farewell letters."

Franzel refers in his Mayerling book to Rudolf's farewell letter to his mother Elisabeth, which has not been preserved: "Nevertheless he wrote to the Empress, in the only letter which he did not write till he was at Mayerling, that he must die, because he has killed. After shooting the devoted girl, who trusted him blindly, he could no longer retreat."

Otto von Habsburg says that, based on the documents given him in 1985, Franzel's version agrees with the circumstances. In saying this, the son of the last Emperor confirms that Rudolf committed

1. Murder (on request) of Mary Vetsera and
2. Suicide.

Concerning the motives, Franzel wrote: "The view prevailed at an early moment that the love story was not the decisive cause of the suicide. It was possibly only a cynical pretext for diverting attention from the true motives."

The Mayerling papers, discovered in the secret archives of the Vatican by Gerd Holler, which Pope John Paul II had published scarcely 100 years after the event, confirm Rudolf's suicide. They contain the correspondence between Emperor Francis Joseph and Pope Leo XLII. In it is a letter dated February 1, 1889, from Luigi Galimberti, who was at that time Papal Nuncio in Vienna, to Rome: "Count Kalnoky (Note:

Imperial Foreign Minister) just came to me to say that Rudolf has committed suicide. However, the University professors and the physicians have stated that the condition of the brain probably indicates a cerebral disorder. The Emperor desires that the Holy Father be informed of this." Of course, the Emperor would not have had the Pope informed of a suicide, if that had not been in accordance with the facts. He was especially eager for his son to receive the blessing of the Church. Suicide only made that difficult. The fiction of a cerebral disease made it possible for the Pope to "wink" at it.

It is out of the question that Emperor Francis Joseph would have allowed his own son to do down in history as a murderer and suicide "because the fate of the Monarchy was at stake," as Zita said, or for whatever reasons, if he had in fact been the victim of an assassination attempt. Even if "the truth had shaken the foundations of the Empire," as Francis Joseph is alleged to have said, the Emperor could not have found it in his heart to tell such a lie. When Archduke Francis Ferdinand was assassinated at Sarajevo in June, 1914, the Emperor went so far as to mobilize for war. And that war cost the Empire millions of human lives and, as we now know, not only "shook its foundations," but destroyed it.

After more than a hundred years, only forensic medicine can determine how Rudolf and Mary really died. At least, insofar as the death of Baroness Vetsera is concerned, after the robbery of the grave at Heiligenkreuz, we now know a lot more . . .

The Skull:
"As to the Question of a Shot . . . "
New Expert Opinions Following the Grave Robbery

When our contract was signed on December 17, 1992, Helmut Flatzelsteiner handed me five official expert opinions. They had been issued in the name of "Theresia Vindona," but we now know that the experts examined in reality the skeleton, skull, shoes and clothing of Baroness Vetsera. Following are the results, published now for the first time:

1. University Professor Dr. Klaus Jarosch, specialist in forensic medicine, 4020 Linz, Humboldt Strasse 18:

"The portions of the skeleton removed from a grave indicate the following: The skeleton is almost complete. Two vertebrae are missing and the lower mandible is not present. It is clearly a human corpse. The vertebrae which are on hand, five cervical vertebrae, ten dorsal vertebrae and five lumbar vertebrae, and the sacrum have not been injured.

With respect to sex, it was observed that there is a pubic angle of 95° and a thigh angle of 130°. This is therefore a female corpse. This is also borne out by the long hair, which have a length of up to 14.8 inches. After cleaning, the color of the hair is light brown.

In addition, there are knock-knees and certain soft parts have been mummified, i.e., the body must have been placed in a relatively warm and aerated environment after death. This occurs in a tomb.

The circumference of the head is 20.8 inches. The skull is in itself small (6 X 6.4 inches).

The skull has been fractured. It is not complete. With respect to a shot, it is to be noted that an aperture on the left beside the eye is possible, with destruction of the skull on the right side, because here there are fragments. In any case, the skull shows fragmentation in many places, which cannot be explained at once. This could have been the cause of death.

There was no particular injury to the ribs, although naturally injuries between the ribs can never be entirely excluded. (Linz, September 11, 1991)"

2. University Professor Dr. Johann Szilvássy. Anthropologist. Sworn expert to the courts. 1090 Vienna, Sensengasse 2.

OPINION

Antecedents: On October 25, 1991, the expert advisor took custody of an almost complete human skeleton. According to a letter from Mr. Helmut Flatzelsteiner, it is the skeleton of the eighteen-year-old Theresia Vindona, who died on May 1, 1891. Allegedly Theresia Vindona died from a shot wound or was stabbed with a knife. Mr. Helmut Flatzelsteiner requested from the expert an opinion for identification and an examination of the skeleton relative to damage inflicted by others.

Result of forensic examination of the skeleton: The skeleton was prepared before the examination and reassembled wherever necessary (for example, the cranium). The examination of the bones submitted showed that this was the skeleton of an eighteen-year-old female person.

Cranium: Brain cover damaged; skull and right area of the skull missing.

Age: The examination indicates an age in life of eighteen to twenty years.

Body height: The size of the long bones indicates a body height of 64.6 inches.

(Vienna, November 20, 1991)"

3. Michael Stolz, M.D., Specialist in Tooth, Mouth and Jaw Surgery, 4020 Linz, Mozart Strasse 5:

OPINION

An osseous lower mandible in two fragments and thirteen teeth (permanent teeth, dentes permanentes), which are partially no longer in their alveoli. Five Röntgen pictures. Both mandible fragments glued together and the loose teeth established in their appropriate osseous alveoli. All teeth show light to medium, brownish discoloration of the enamel. There is no evidence of tartar development. However, slight lesions and discolorations at the border of the enamel between the root and the crown support the hypothesis of previous film. This is a narrow lower jawbone.

According to the X-rays, all of the teeth must have been alive at the time of death. No root surgery is visible in any tooth. In tooth number 4, caries extends as far as the pulp. Eventually that tooth would probably have caused pain in the pulp.

Conclusion: This is the lower mandible of an apparently female young adult between the ages of 14 and 25 years. Slight periodontic problems, little minor caries and good preservative care indicate a relatively good dental condition and healthy nutrition, good mouth hygiene and proper care by a dentist. (Linz, August, 1991.)"

4. Austrian Institute for Textile Research, State-approved Testing Agency for Textiles. 1050 Vienna, Spengergasse 20.

OPINION

Classification of the testing sample: Women's clothing Cloth—100 years old. On September 5, 1991, we received 1 piece of women's clothing, 100 years old according to the requester. It was found by examination that this testing sample in warp and woof consists of 100 o/o wool, that it is a part-linen weave which has been dressed. Due to the fineness of the yarn, it may be assumed to be a worsted . . . Today, this type of weave would be classified as "worsted flannel". (Vienna, October 1, 1991)"

5. Professor Dr. Annemarie Bönsch, Institute for Costume Studies, College for Applied Art, 1010 Vienna, (Oskar Kokoschka Platz 2.

Dear Mr. Flatzelsteiner! We had to get up courage to work in detail on the clothing of your great-grandmother. Frau

Carmen Bock, who does restoration for us, took on this difficult work, so that I was able to determine the time of origin of the piece of clothing from a few existing details. We found diagonal pleats in the front part of the skirt, which indicate 1889/90. The bulk and style of the rear pleated part confirm this hypothesis. The upper part is a jacket with a short coattail, where the real silk lining leads one to assume a narrow shoulder seam, which likewise belong to that time. We were able to identify the label of the Fischer Company on the inner lining of the jacket. It was removed and steamed for purposes of legibility. Perhaps it was a winter or ice skating costume, since Josef Fischer specialized in athletic clothing.

Regarding the material, we concluded the following, based on our experience:

Jacket: Silk plush, lining rep silk; we could not find any other pieces of material. There were no clasps or reinforcing materials.

Skirt: Silk fabric. Hems reinforced with silk ribbons by hand, many seams were also handsewn. In the lower third of the skirt was a facing of several layers with woolen edging.

Stockings: silk thread, machinemade.

Shoes: Leather pumps with rep silk lining, trimmed with silk ribbon, a cork piece in the heel section of the sole, curved, leathercovered heel, metal reinforcement in the sole to support the high heel, soft leather sole.

Fur remains: in very poor condition. No article of clothing is recognizable, possibly a hat or muff.

Color: No residue of color could be found, since all parts were covered with the typical fashion color (Brown) It is possible that the material of the skirt was preserved in a beige tone. The colors of the jacket and the lining may have been different.

Frau Bock has wrapped the remains of the clothing in acid-free paper and suggests leaving them in it and not folding the pieces any smaller. The parcel with the remains of the clothing was mailed to you at the same time!

(Vienna, October 8, 1991)"

Obviously, these five expert opinions were drawn up before it was known that this was the body of Mary Vetsera and that these were her clothes. Now I asked certain of the scientists who were to explain the case to comment on those findings for this book.

As far as Professor Szilvássy is concerned, there is "no doubt that the 'Theresia Vindona' whom he examined was really Mary Vetsera." This was proven by the so-called "superprojection," in which an original profile photograph of the Baroness over a profile picture of the skull that was discovered is compared in a phototechnical process. The result is clear. Regarding the cause of death, Professor Bankl said:

"As the skull has been blown up into pieces and had to be reassembled by both experts (Jarosch and Szilvássy), we are in the presence of an act of violence the probability of which is nearly certain. The wound from a shot typically results in the dissolution of the skull into fragments. Hence, in view of the present stage of the examination of the death of Mary Vetsera, a shot in the head must be assumed." This confirms the postmortem finding by the Imperial house physician Dr. Auchenthaler on January 31, 1889.

Professor Annemarie Bönsch on the clothing: "The historical data, according to which Mary Vetsera was buried in a tightfitting costume with cord embroidery, are identical with the results of our examination of the clothing."

"No Danger that Rudolf Would Be an Exemplary Husband"
The Crown Prince and Women

"Love is certainly the most beautiful thing in
the life of all organic beings. It is a feeling that
humans possess as clearly as animals; in it,
they are still completely in harmony with
Nature."

Crown Prince Rudolf,
"Einzelne Gedanken," 1875.

It is absolutely certain that Mary Vetsera was not the "great
love" of Crown Prince Rudolf's life. The Crown Prince was
involved in so many affairs, which even ran concurrently. Mary
Vetsera was not even the first and only woman with whom he
wanted to die. "Who was Vetsera?" Crown Princess Stephanie
recalled contemptuously in her memoirs. "One of many. He
spent his last night with his friend, Vienna's Grande Cocotte."
This referred to Mizzy Caspar. How close she was to him
is shown by the fact that in his will, Rudolf wrote: "Whatever
money remains, give everything to Mizzy Caspar. My
chamberlain Loschek is well acquainted with her address."
Earlier, the Crown Prince had incurred heavy debts in order
to please Mizzy Caspar. He had given her valuable jewelry
and a house on the Wieden, where he spent many a night,
including the last one, before he went to Mayerling.
Maria Caspar was born in Graz on September 28, 1864
and was twenty-two years old when her relationship with the
Emperor's son began. She referred to herself in official papers
as a "soubrette" or "dancer," but it is out of the question that
the dark-haired beauty was ever really active in that profession;
in any case, her name does not appear in the cast of any
Austrian theater.
Her affair with the Crown Prince of Austria-Hungary began

in 1886, three years after Mizzy Caspar came to Vienna from Styria. As often in the past, Rudolf had asked the well-known matchmaker Wolf to find some feminine change for his life. Wolf, who had the most beautiful women of the demimonde in Vienna under her control, supplied many partners to the Crown Prince, as she did for many other members of the Imperial house, and always received a very good honorarium for so doing.

We owe detailed descriptions of the relationship of the Habsburg prince to the attractive woman from Graz to detectives of the Imperial Police Institute, who sniffed about Rudolf's private life during the months before Mayerling "for the sake of his security." For example: "Mizi said the K.R. (Note: Crown Prince Rudolf) was impotent and only capable of coitus when he had drunk champagne."

It is also informative to note this from the police records about Rudolf's view of Austro-Hungarian politics: "Crown Prince Rudolf told Mizi: "The government is going to hell and Franzl (Note: Archduke Francis Ferdinand) must carry it on." So the Crown Prince could quite imagine that one day not he, but his cousin, would have to succeed Emperor Francis Joseph, apparently because he would not outlive his father.

Caspar had a presentiment of that too. Half a year before the actual suicide, he suggested to Mizzy shooting himself with her in front of the Temple of the Hussars in Mödling. When the frightened mistress went to the Chief of Police, Baron Krauss, to report that to him, he placed the Crown Prince under stricter surveillance than before. Rudolf's movements were watched day and night by police detectives.

Here is an excerpt from the reports of the Imperial Police Institute: "K.R. said to Mizi repeatedly—after the summer of 1888—that his honor demanded that he shoot himself. He did not explain in greater detail why his honor demanded it." But above all, it remains a mystery how it was compatible with Rudolf's honor to want to take an innocent young person with him to death.

One thing is certain: The police had known for a long time

from Mizzy Caspar's statements about the situation threatening the life of the Crown Prince. And they were unable to save him or to warn those nearest him of the impending catastrophe. Not only did the Crown Prince spend the night regularly at Mizzy's house at Heumühlgasse 10, but also openly compromised his wife with the woman of doubtful reputation" as she was known at Court. Rudolf's aide-de-camp, Count Maximilian Orsini-Rosenberg, made an affidavit to the effect that during his last two years of life, the Crown Prince had even taken Mizzy Caspar with him on military inspection trips, much to the displeasure of his closest companions, and Mizzy was also seen at their night quarters."

The story which is often repeated that the Crown Prince died because of his ill-fated love for Baroness Vetsera is certainly false. Rudolf's grandson, Prince Francis Joseph Windisch-Graetz once said: "It has been proven that my grandfather had more than thirty illegitimate children. What chutzpah to insinuate that the heir to one of the most powerful empires in the world shot himself because of a teenager!"

Count Hoyos, the Crown Prince's hunting partner, also declared in his memorandum that in the tragic days of January, 1889, the relationship between Rudolf and Mary had already cooled. Mizzy Caspar was much closer to him. The Crown Prince was attached to her as always. Among his many love-affairs, she was without doubt the one in whom he had most confidence, who was closest to him.

Mary was not even the only Vetsera who had fallen in love with him. Twelve years before her time, Rudolf had had an impetuous affair with Mary's mother. Baroness Helene Vetsera, whose husband, as a professional diplomat, was seldom in Vienna, was eleven years older than the Crown Prince and is said to have taken the initiative in that relationship with great energy. She was described as a "small, delicate person with unforgettable blue-gray eyes and beautiful long eyelashes, which lent a special, strange expression to her fine face." The southern beauty belonged to the type of woman whom the Crown Prince even later favored above others. Her dark hair and dark eyes contrasted with her silky-white skin in a way that caused infatuation of the onlooker. Mary was just six years old at the time of her mother's liaison with Rudolf.

Until his marriage, Rudolf was one of the most sought after bachelors, not only in Austria-Hungary, but in all Europe. The twenty-year-old Princess Catherine Radziwill described him as follows: "He was not exactly a handsome young man, but still unusually attractive. His youthful face was very serious, which made him appear much older, and his reddish hair was decidedly repulsive, but his eyes had a dreamy expression, full of mystery and passion, which gained the goodwill of everyone with whom he spoke. Rudolf made an impression that was quite different from what one expected and a certain staccato way of speaking caused one to wonder what reasons there were for his impatience and dissatisfaction. His manners were extremely courteous, but nevertheless rather cool and had a trace of disdain in them."

But the little girls of the middle class also had crushes on their "fairy prince," according to the memoirs of the celebrated actress Rosa Albach-Retty (1874-1980): "In those days, we teenagers of the Stekkel School for Girls had crushes on Crown Prince Rudolf just as the fourteen-year-olds of now have crushes on their film and television favorites. We carried his picture around in our school bags like a treasure."

Rudolf was able to exploit that admiration to the full. He had many love affairs from his earliest youth on, among which was one with Johanna Buska, an actress in the Burgtheater, who is said to have been his first "great love." This was a situation characteristic of an aristocrat in the second half of the nineteenth century: A young man from a wealthy family enters into a "relationship" with a woman who is experienced in sexual practices. This is supposed to prepare the future gallant for his later love life. At that time, such arrangements were mostly made by the parents. For this training, artists could be obtained for an appropriate fee and also prostitutes, as well as serving girls or children's nannies. Naturally it was not necessary for the parents to participate personally in the "happiness" of their son at the Imperial Court. A man of the world par excellence had been found in Count Charles Bombelles who, a Head Chamberlain to the Crown Prince, had to see to it that Rudolf's adventures had proper variety. It is not surprising that sexuality at that time had very little to do with love.

At the time of the Crown Prince's puberty, feminine eroticism was undergoing considerable change. It was precisely in the seventies that the crinolines that concealed all the charms disappeared; breasts and hips were emphasized, low necklines permitted views which had not been dared before; naked arms were shown as a big sensation. Women could suddenly be lascivious, provocative and self-assured and they mastered the art of flirting. The new, curled hairdressing also proved seductive.

In addition to the Crown Prince's "education" to be a hero among the women, the "marriage policy" common then among the ruling houses was probably one of the main reasons for the Crown Prince's polygamous conduct. Marriage was not for love, but for *raison d'état*.

The marriage with Princess Stephanie, the daughter of King Leopold II of Belgium, was condemmed to failure from the start. When Rudolf traveled to Brussels to ask for her hand in marriage, a mistress—also from the theater—was part of the staff that accompanied the Emperor's son. This also caused an embarrassing scene, when Queen Marie Henriette, the bride's mother, paid an unexpected courtesy call on her future son-in-law at his quarters in Brussels. There she found him in the arms of the mistress he had brought with him from Vienna. The wedding almost blew up because of that.

Stephanie was neither beautiful nor well educated; she had neither charm nor grace. It was only important, according to Habsburg laws, that she was of equal rank, i.e., came from a Catholic royal house. The choice was quite limited in that respect, for the House of Austria was already related by blood or marriage over and over again to nearly all of the families concerned. They did not want to "risk" a Bavarian princess again, for the blood relationships were too close and the intellectual degeneration was too evident in the Bavarian King Ludwig II and his brother Otto, who lived in a hospital for the insane.

The Crown Prince, already spoiled by willing, beautiful girls, first went to "inspect" the Saxon Princess Mathilde. And he had scarcely seen her when he returned to Vienna in horror. Mathilde was fat, shapeless and awkward. As he went looking for a bride, he was just as little attracted to the Spanish infanta or to several princesses of the Houses of Orléans, Bourbon or Portugal.

Although Stephanie of Belgium was in no way his "type," Rudolf had to decide for better or for worse during his visit to Brussels in favor of that homely, pale girl with dun-colored blond hair. The engagement was a farce, the introduction lasted a short five minutes. Rudolf saw his bride for the first time at an intimate family dinner. Stephanie recalls it in her memoirs: "The Crown Prince entered. He wore the uniform of an Austrian colonel with the Grand Cross of the Order of Saint Stephen and the Golden Fleece. I was beside myself with excitement and I thought people could see my heart beat through the clothes. After the prince had bowed and been greeted by all members of the family, he drew near to me. My father introduced him to me with a few kind words. The prince's manner was accomplished and self-assured. He kissed my hand, spoke to me in German and said a few flattering, but formal, things; after only a few minutes, he asked me the big question, which would decide our future. Then he gave me his arm and we approached my parents, asking them to bless our engagement. They joyfully kissed their future son-in-law and permitted us henceforth to say "du" to each other."

Whereas Rudolf, the son of the first monarch of Europe, must have seemed to the Belgians a "good match," Stephanie was less attractive, even from the aristocratic side. King Leopold, whose many shady business transactions had caused controversy, was labeled by many people as a parvenu. Elisabeth was opposed to her son's marriage to this princess, who was only fifteen years old, from the beginning. She considered her unsuited, both physically and from the point of view of character, to occupy a place beside the future sovereign of a world empire.

The Empress was in England when she learned of Rudolf's engagement. She grew pale when she read the telegram containing the news that Stephanie of Belgium was the chosen one. Countess Marie Festetics, standing beside the Empress, asked her anxiously for God's sake what had happened. When the lady-in-waiting learned that Rudolf had become engaged, she gave a sigh of relief and said she had thought there might have been a catastrophe. Elisabeth answered sadly: "Please God there will not be one!"

The Empress pointedly remained in Brussels for only two hours to make the acquaintance of her future daughter-in-law. The contrast between the "most beautiful woman in Europe", as the forty-two-year-old Elisabeth was still considered, and the "ugly duckling" from Belgium was striking and must have impressed all who were present at the festive reception for the Empress. Rudolf and Stephanie were married on May 10, 1881, at the Augustiner Church in Vienna. Observers noted that Rudolf's quiet, resigned "ja" was in flagrant contrast to the loud, strong answer given by the bride to the question of Cardinal Prince Frederick zu Schwarzenberg of Prague, who was assisted at the ceremony by twenty-four bishops and archbishops.

The wedding night at Laxenburg Castle was a first-class fiasco. Stephanie had not been prepared at all and Rudolf attacked her in the brutal conqueror's manner to which he was accustomed from his many love affairs. Fifty years later, Stephanie would write of that, for her, frightful experience: "What a night! What agony, what loathing! I knew nothing. They led me to the altar as an unsuspecting child. My illusions, the dreams of my youth were destroyed. I felt that I must die of my disappointment."

Yet it seemed at first as though the two might turn out to be happy with each other. Before the wedding, the Crown

Prince had written euphorically to his cousin, King Ludwig of Bavaria: "I have found a real angel in Stephanie, a sincere, good person who loves me; an intelligent, cultured, clever companion for life, who will stand beside me well in all my duties."

Writing to his tutor Latour (who had often criticized him as a child for lying), he pretended in a letter shortly after the wedding: "I am very much in love with her and she is the only one who could lead me astray in many things!" Quite to the contrary, Rudolf's dissolute "love" life was to become still more intense during the short eight years of his marriage. "Love" in quotation marks, because the affairs, partly among prostitutes, had little to do with love. He must have been scarcely capable of genuine, deep love. For this, as we know since Sigmund Freud, the roots probably lay in Rudolf's childhood.

Stephanie wrote in her memoirs: "The Crown Prince was used to having no female creature stand in his way." Marie Larisch stated the dilemma this way in her autobiographical notes: "With that wife, there was no danger that Rudolf would be an exemplary husband."

He probably would not have become one otherwise.

While his political isolation plunged the successor to the throne deeper and deeper into depression, Stephanie began to enjoy her position as future empress. Particularly after the birth of her daughter Elisabeth and after they had all moved from Prague to Vienna, she behaved in a conceited and arrogant manner, happy to make a show. Archduke Leopold Salvator, who later left the Imperial House and took the name Leopold Wölfling, observed: "Stephanie appeared as a 'cool blonde,' always correct on the outside, very refined and very gracious, but it was unmistakable that that film was a mask for a dissatisfied personality; in private, one never crossed the barrier of affected conventionality . . . Rudolf would have lived better with an apathetic wife than with a volcano covered by an ice cap." According to Leopold Wölfling, Rudolf was married to the "wrong woman." In fact, she had no understanding for her husband's numerous intellectual interests nor for his liberal political ideas. Thinking in an ultraconservative manner, her entire horizon extended no farther than to preserving the existing system with all the representational duties and comfort it offered her. In Rudolf and Stephanie, two worlds had come into conflict.

After a few years of vehement infidelity, the Crown Princess gave her husband as good as she got. Her long-lasting liaison with Count Arthur Potocki, whom she called "the great love" of her life, and whom she met regularly at Abbazia, has been proven. But her relationship with the Polish aristocrat was probably not the only one during Stephanie's marriage.

Whereas Stephanie was able to keep her love affairs secret, during the Crown Prince's last years, people knew of his countless affairs throughout all parts of the Monarchy. And so he had to accept many attacks by his opponents.

Schönerer's followers compared the "immoral, Jew-loving adulterer" Rudolf in foreign newspapers to the "Christian, blameless Crown Prince of Germany." In this judgment they were unjust, for the later German Emperor Wilhelm II found amusement, when in Vienna, like Rudolf, among the lambs of Madame Wolf. This was arranged by none other then the Austrian successor to the throne, for whom the beauties of the night also rendered service as informants. Rudolf wrote to the Austrian chargé d'affaires in Berlin, Colonel Karl von Steininger, that while in his cups in the brothel, Wilhelm "did not speak quite respectfully of our Emperor", "and unfavorably of me." He said "things are only going right in Prussia; in Austria, the whole country is rotten and close to dissolution. If the Austrian Emperor wishes, he can continue his life as an insignificant monarch in Hungary. Prussia will not do anything to bring that about, as it will very soon come by itself in any case."

Rudolf was hindered more and more in his duties as military commander by his amorous adventures. The art historian Eduard Leisching recalls in his notes concerning the maneuvers of 1887/88, in which he participated as a young officer: "At Bruck, he (Note: Rudolf) resided at the castle and was to head the 'exercises of opposing parties' every day at 6 or 7 in the morning. However, he often did not come at the appointed time to the field of operations, or not at all, and there was a lot of open talk among the officers that there had been wild drinking all night long at the castle in small or large groups (including 'ladies'), which made the Crown Prince unable to leave his quarters, where he had gone at a late hour or probably not at all . . . "

Rudolf's relationship with the other sex appears as early as in his first will, drawn up in 1879. "A last farewell," it ran, "in memory of all the beautiful women of Vienna, whom I loved so much."

"He Was More Modern Than Most Habsburgs"
Visit with Rudolf's Great-Grandson

Guillaume Windisch-Graetz, the great-grandson of the Crown Prince, is 43 years old and lives in Vienna. Rudolf's only daughter, Archduchess Elisabeth, had four children, three of whom died relatively early and only her eldest son Francis Joseph left direct descendants. Guillaume is the only son of Prince Francis Joseph Windisch-Graetz and is thereby the head of the family after Rudolf. I visited the prince at the Palais Windisch-Graetz in the Strohgasse in Vienna.

The Crown Prince's progressive ideas are continuing here in the elegant atmosphere of the fine family home. If the Habsburgs were divided into a conservative and liberal wing, Rudolf's descendant belongs without a doubt to the latter group. But whoever thinks he will find in Guillaume Windisch-Graetz a glowing admirer of his great-grandfather will be disappointed. "Yes, I also have rather progressive ideas," declared the prince, "and so I am able to admire my great-grandfather's political views, but there are also immense reservations. In my opinion, he paid too little attention to the economic and social conditions in the monarchy and concentrated too much on foreign policy. But above all, one must evaluate the character of the Crown Prince and of course one cannot forget what he did at Mayerling."

Guillaume Windisch-Graetz is convinced that his great-grandfather shot Mary Vetsera and then committed suicide.

In his view, "the Crown Prince had six classical reasons for killing himself: a troubled relationship with his mother, who scarcely cared for him; the bad relationship with his father; his catastrophic marriage; his many love affairs, none of which led to fulfillment; his bad health, and the frustration of his political objectives."

He said that Rudolf was ahead of his time in his outlook. "And I can well imagine that he could have saved the monarchy. He would probably have been able to solve the

87

nationality problem; he would have created a federal state and have agreed to regional autonomy. He would have raised the Czechs to the same level as the Hungarians. He would have dealt with the Serbian problem and would have introduced universal suffrage sooner than Francis Joseph. He was simply much more modern than his father and most of the other Habsburgs," declared Guillaume Windisch-Graetz, who referred to himself as an "ardent republican."

In spite of all his esteem for the political opinions and activities of his great-grandfather, the prince rejected his personality altogether. "He was a total failure as a human being, as a husband, as a son and father."

Besides valuable furniture and many pictures in which one can recognize famous ancestors, they showed me at Palais Windisch-Graetz a rather simple, brightly lacquered toilet table with a large mirror. "Without doubt, Mary Vetsera looked at herself in that mirror for the last time, when she removed the pins from her coiffure and let her hair fall loosely over her shoulders, as she was found later after her death. Two small tags hanging on the keys bore the words "Mayerling Room" and thus confirmed the origin of the furniture," explained Ghislaine Windisch-Graetz, my host's mother, who has also written a highly-regarded book about her mother-in-law, Archduchess Elisabeth.

Even though Rudolf's great-grandson has no doubt about the double suicide at Mayerling, Guillaume Windisch-Graetz would "immediately consent" to exhumation of the Crown Prince. For only if the circumstances are all known "will the constant speculations about Mayerling come to rest. With the present status of the inquiries, the public is not convinced, even after more than a century, how Rudolf and Mary really died."

Guillaume Windisch-Graetz pointed out that this was an entirely personal opinion, because, on the basis of family laws (which are of course not laws in the meaning of civil jurisprudence), the decision as to whether Rudolf should be exhumed or not does not lie with the Crown Prince's direct descendants, but rather with the head of the family, Otto von Habsburg, and with the Capuchin friars. All previous requests for exhumation of Rudolf have been refused.

A Strange Hunting Accident
Did Rudolf Intend to Kill the Emperor?

The hunting accident occurred on January 3, 1888, one year before Mayerling. This strange affair was likewise never entirely explained. In the area of the Imperial hunting lodge at Mürzsteg, Crown Prince Rudolf fired a shot which missed his father, Emperor Francis Joseph, by only a hair's breadth. A park custodian was wounded. This is the question: Was it really an accident? Or an attempt at assassination? In any case, the Crown Prince's grandson believed that Rudolf intended to kill the Emperor.

First of all: Almost the only thing that attached the Crown Prince to his father was the love of hunting. Francis Joseph had trained Rudolf at an early age to be a hunter and when he was a small child had had a short hunting rifle made for him by a gunsmith in Ischl named Leithner. At the end of August, 1867, *Hugo's Hunting News* reported under the headline "The Crown Prince's First Hunt on the Gaisberg" that on the 22nd of that month, Crown Prince Rudolf had skilfully slain a stag with ten points.—When Colonel Latour urged the Crown Prince to aim at a chamois, he did so, but put down his gun and said calmly to the colonel: "It is a kid." The colonel only discovered the kid after long observation.

The places Rudolf preferred were Court hunts at Goisern and Ebensee, the castle park at Schönbrunn, the zoological park at Lainz, Aspern, Laxenburg, the hunts in the high mountains of the Salzkammergut and the foothills of Styria. In these, he surpassed his father in Auerhahn shooting (Note: a kind of wild turkey) at sixteen and had shot his hundredth chamois at eighteen. *Hugo's Hunting News* mentioned as a particular feat that on December 16, 1881, the Crown Prince had felled ninety-six wild boars in only two hours at the Lainz zoölogical garden. During his career of about twenty years as a hunter, the shooting lists show that he had an overall total of 43,565 wild animals shot, but it was expressly stipulated that the number was incomplete and that the actual total was probably around 50,000.

The hunting accident at Mürzsteg has been proven and was described in 1928 by Oskar von Mitis in the first large biography of Rudolf which he had written: "The shot by the successor to the throne only missed his father by a hair's breadth . . . when they were hunting young deer at Höllgraben near Mürzsteg. After both the Emperor and the Crown Prince had fired a lot, and the beating was already ending, another herd of game approached the prince. He shot at the herd and when it fled and became less accessible to him, he forgot the old rule, left his stand and fired again as the game was already approaching the Emperor's stand. The ball struck the bearer Martin Veitschegger, who was sitting behind the Emperor's stand, in his sleeve near the elbow. He received 50 guilders from the Emperor and the Crown Prince was not allowed to participate in the beating on the following day. Thus, the danger of a shocking catastrophe, which would have had unforeseeable consequences, was caused by the Crown Prince's entirely abnormal behavior . . . "

The only version of this that ever existed was that of an accident. Until, in August, 1988, the writer Rolf Hochhuth published in an article in the Viennese *Presse* half a year before the Mayerling centenary a conversation he had had with the grandson of the Crown Prince, who died in 1981.

Hochhuth wrote that once he had been the guest of Prince Francis Joseph Windisch-Graetz (the father of Guillaume Windisch-Graetz mentioned in the preceding chapter). As might be expected, the conversation between Windisch-Graetz and Hochhuth soon turned to Mayerling. Suddenly the prince said to the writer: "One does not like to say it as a grandson, but my grandfather shot at the Emperor! He tried to kill him during a hunt, but the shot hit the arm of the man loading the gun. Just as he was holding out a newly-loaded gun to the Emperor, he was struck in the left underarm. Chalk-white, the Emperor came down from his shooting position and before all who had gathered around he ordered his son to leave the hunt at once. The fact that the Crown Prince had set up his stand at that place pointed to an assassination attempt. One does not position oneself in such a way that one can so easily hit one's neighbor . . . "

The grandson was convinced that there had been no "hunting accident," as Rudolf was an expert marksman: it was an attempt at assassination. According to Hochhuth, Windisch-Graetz was "entirely above any suspicion of accusing his grandfather of an attempt on the life of his great-grandfather in a frivolous, unproven way. The prince saw in his grandfather an important politician who was frustrated at not being able to bring about any reform to save the monarchy because of his inflexible father and was therefore constrained to violent opposition even to the point of an attempted assassination." "This," Rolf Hochhuth added to his report, "I wanted to communicate."

At this point we should also add the passage from one of Rudolf's letters to Stéphanie, which has already been mentioned. He wrote about the German Emperor, whom he detested: "At most I should like to invite Wilhelm, in order to get rid of him by a hunting accident . . . "

That letter was written in 1888, the same year in which that mysterious hunting accident took place!

Guillaume Windisch-Graetz confirmed that his father's conversation with Hochhuth had taken place, and he also said that his father, in contrast with himself, in fact believed that Rudolf had tried to kill the Emperor.

So up to that point I could follow Rolf Hochhuth. However, I cannot understand the conclusion he draws from the hunting episode as explained by Rudolf's grandson.

In reference to Mayerling, the Emperor has often been quoted as saying: "My son died like a Schneider." In hunters' parlance, which Francis Joseph often used, a "Schneider" is a cowardly stag that withdraws, facing the people: a weakling, a coward. Hochhuth concludes that if Rudolf had committed suicide, according to the code of honor of the Imperial officers, he would not have been a coward. He says that the Crown Prince killed Mary, but was then too cowardly to carry out his original plan to shoot himself after his mistress's death. So, according to Hochhuth, he asked an officer to shoot him. It was because Rudolf lacked the courage to accept the consequences of his horrible deed that the Emperor called him a "Schneider," a weakling.

Another version. Of course, there is too much against it. The "hunting accident" is still worth reporting.

Baroness Mary Vetsera

Mary's parents, Albert Freiherr von Vetsera and Helene von Vetsera, née Baltazzi.

Mary Vetsera as a schoolgirl in the "Institute for Daughters of the Nobility."

Palais Vetsera, residence of Albert and Helene von Vetsera in Salesianergasse 11, Vienna. It later became Palais Salm.

Some of the "many faces" of Maria
Vetsera, showing her interest in
costume and fashion.

Crown Prince Rudolf von Habsburg-Lothringen in Austrian military uniform wearing the insignia of the Golden Fleece.

Baroness Mary Vetsera in 1888 when her liaison with the Crown Prince Rudolf began.

Emperor Francis Joseph and Empress Elisabeth in the 1850s.

Maria ("Mizzy") Caspar, the foremost of Rudolf's many mistresses, who twice refused his suggestion to die with him.

Archduke Rudolf with his wife, Princess Stéphanie of Belgium.

A drawing made shortly after the trajedy at Mayerling, showing Rudolf and Mary in a carriage driven by Bratfisch. The "fiaker" is a closed carriage; this is a variant of the *calèche*, which is open.

The Crown Prince's hunting Lodge at Mayerling in 1889, which was rebuilt as a Carmelite cloister after the tragedy.

The Linz furniture dealer Helmut Flatzelsteiner, who wanted to solve the "Mayerling puzzle."

Flatzelsteiner's attorneys Adolf (left) and Alfred Kriegler (right) with Helmut Flatzelsteiner.

Dr. Franz Auchenthaler, the Court physician who made the post mortem examinations at Mayerling and issued the death certificate.

Dr. Hans Bankl, pathologist.

Dr. Johann Szilvássy, anthropologist.

Dr. Georg Bauer, head of the Viennese Institute of Forensic Medicine.

Crown Prince Rudolf's great-grandson Guillaume Windisch-Graetz and a toilet table from Mayerling.

Rudolf's only daughter, Elisabeth, known as the "red archduchess."

Rudolf in the hunting costume he wore to Mayerling.

Mary Vetsera in the hat, muff and sport costume which were later found in her grave at Heiligenstadt.

Countess Marie Louise Larisch, niece of Empress Elisabeth, who arranged the meetings between Mary and Rudolf.

Josef Bratfisch, singer of Viennese popular songs and personal coachman of the Crown Prince, drove Rudolf and Mary to Mayerling on January 28, 1889.

The Mayerling star witness, Johann Loschek.

Count Joseph Hoyos, Rudolf's hunting companion.

The Crown Prince, lying in state in his bedroom at the Hofburg.

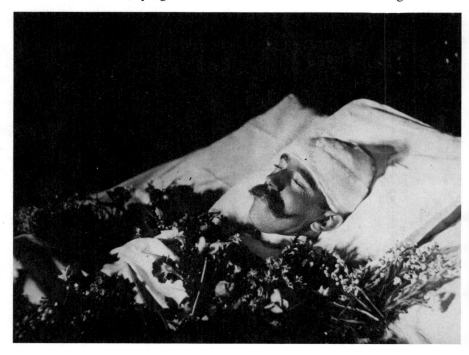

Mary's grave at Heiligenkreuz was officially opened on December 22, 1992, and was found empty. She has since been reinterred there.

Rudolf and the Schrammeln[4]
The Crown Prince Composes Viennese Songs

It was during hunting excursions that Rudolf met the two men who would be the star witnesses to the tragic events at Mayerling: the hunt assistant and later chamberlain Loschek and his personal coachman Bratfisch. "It was on September 30, 1877, in the Imperial preserve of Auhof, where I was assigned," Johann Loschek recalled, in his memoirs, the first meeting with the Crown Prince. "The Empress Elisabeth and Rudolf drove up and asked me for a glass of water, which I gave them. I noticed that the Empress looked me up and down from head to foot. On the next day I received my appointment and henceforth I was with Rudolf at the Hofburg, in whose enormous rooms I soon received good orientation. Now I was with Rudolf until his death at Mayerling. I went on the long trips and thus became Rudolf's confidant. At the time of the drama at Mayerling, I was supposed to have other duty. But Rudolf gave me the order: 'Loschek, come with me to Mayerling.' But I could not imagine what would happen." The strangest friendship of the successor to the throne developed during another hunting excursion: his friendship with the singing coachman Josef Bratfisch.

At that time, the Schrammeln were the most popular music group in Vienna. The brothers Johann and Josef Schrammel and Anton Strohmayer and Georg Dänzer had created immortal songs like "Wien bleibt Wien" "'s Herz von an echten Weana" or "Vindobona, du herrliche Stadt." In 1887 the quartet played regularly at the restaurant "Zur goldenen Waldschnepfe" in Dornbach, in front of which there were often three hundred carriages waiting till the late evening hours to return the noble

---

[4] Kaspar Schrammel (1811-1885) and his sons Johann (1850-1893) and Josef (1852-1895) were popular composers of Viennese folk songs.

and music-loving clientele to the inner sections of the city. Crown Prince Rudolf was also one of the guests. In early November of that year, Johann Schrammel received a letter from the famous composer and conductor Carl Michael Ziehrer, who was acting as an advisor to the successor to the throne in matters of popular music. "Dear Mr. Schrammel," wrote Ziehrer, "between the 14th and 17th of this month, a genuine Viennese evening is to be held for His Imperial Highness the Crown Prince. I am coming to ask you if you would have time to play on those days (in the evening), naturally with several of your singers. Kindly favor me with your visit between 1 and 2 tomorrow, as I must report on this in the evening. C. M. Ziehrer, III. District, Gärtnergasse 17."

In Vienna, people had known for a long time of the Crown Prince's enthusiasm for popular songs. He was often seen, sometimes recognized, sometimes incognito, in restaurants and little bars, where he listened for hours on end with close attention to the "schmalzig" (sentimental) lyrics of the musicians. Of course, this evening was to be something special.

And so the Schrammel quartet drummed up the best Heurigen singers of Vienna, in order to offer the Crown Prince's hunting society at Castle Orth on the Danube something out of the ordinary. In addition to the Schrammels were, among others, the coachmen-singers Bratfisch and Hungerl, the flutist "Baron Jean," the yodeler "Kiesel Marie," the "Hairdresser Brady" and the innkeeper and bagpipe player Josef Brandmeyer from Grinzing.

There was also a black among them who worked at the Kreipl Hotel and, like all the singers, musicians and helpers, was lodged during the time of the Crown Prince's hunting reception at an inn nearby. In that connection an episode has come down to us about a farmer's wife on whose premises the black bartender was to spend the night. When he arrived, she asked a cobbler who was traveling with him "if that was the black's real color." "Don't believe it," he answered jokingly, "we only painted him that way." And to prove it, he dipped his index finger secretly into the grease of a wheel hub, passed it over the Negro's cheek and showed his black finger. The woman gave a horrified shriek and ran off to change the fresh, white bedding for her oldest covers which had been mended a hundred times.

The first music was heard at Orth Castle on the day of arrival, in the presence of the Crown Prince and Crown Princess, and also of Archduke Francis Ferdinand, Prince Leopold in Bavaria and Philip of Coburg, according to a report in the *Illustriertes Extrablatt*, with the gentlemen in dress coats and the ladies in walking clothes. The lively party lasted from six in the evening till three in the morning "and both the musicians and singers were enthusiastically applauded by the high-ranking guests."

The next day, Rudolf was again lucky in the hunt and shot a sixteen-point stag. Johann Schrammel took that as a theme for a march he then composed which he entitled "Jagdabenteuer" (hunting adventure). Dedicated to the Crown Prince, it was played on the second evening at Orth Castle. According to the *Extrablatt*, the Crown Prince always "gave the signal for applause, was in high spirits and afterwards asked Bratfisch for the song "Das waß nur a Weana, a weanerisches Blut." The coachman knew the melody, but not the words, so the Crown Prince took paper and wrote the lines of the song down from memory and gave the paper to the coachman."

Josef Bratfisch as Entertainer

The *Extrablatt* did not report what happened then. Bratfisch could only read the cursive handwriting customary at that time and could not understand Ruldolf's Latin letters. He objected, with complete neglect of the customarily strict rules governing contact with members of the Imperial family: "No decent person can read such writing!" Rudolf laughed heartily at that outburst of temper, put his arm around the forty-two-year-old coachman, called him "Du" and sang in duet with him the beloved Viennese song "Das is in Weana sein Schan." Then he appointed him on the spot to be his personal coachman.

Although the Crown Prince had given his word while under

the influence of wine, he held to it in spite of all scruples and prejudices. He continued a friendly relationship with Bratfisch and took him into the confidence of his love affairs. Rudolf also repaid the singing coachman in a princely way for his faithful service: he purchased a small house in Hernals for him and frequently visited him there. Once, in the autumn of 1888, he even came there with "Fräulein Mitzi Kaspar," as Bratfisch's daughter Antonia Konhäuser later wrote. She said that "the Crown Prince came particularly at teatime because of the garnished Liptauer which my mother made extraordinarily well in his opinion and which he never had in that way at Court. With that we drank beer and some wine."[5]

The Viennese experienced a thrill after the parties at Orth Castle. The fact that the Emperor's son showed so openly his attachment to the popular songs contributed a great deal toward increasing their attachment to the successor to the throne, who had been a favorite of theirs for a long time anyway. On the other hand, loud voices were heard at the Court, making fun of the fact that the Crown Prince had gone decidedly too far in his contact with the simple people and had given evidence of a preference which was incompatible with his station. There was also shocked whispering in private about the scene of fraternization between the Crown Prince and the coachman.

There were other Schrammel evenings for Rudolf at Laxenburg and at the Mayerling hunting lodge, which was to be the site of the tragedy one year later. The often-repeated story that the Schrammel quartet had played for Rudolf and Mary on the evening preceding their death is indeed only a legend. One of those who could not comprehend Rudolf's predilection for Viennese songs and the Heurigen singers was

---

[5] Liptauer is a Slovak sheep cheese, named for the Liptauer Alps in the Slovak section of the Carpathian Mountains.

the Emperor.[6] A few months after his son's death, the Schrammel musicians were asked to play for an evening at the home of the Court actress Katharina Schratt in the Gloriettegasse opposite the Schönbrunn Palace. As they were often engaged to play for private parties, this was not surprising for them at first, but this time they did not find a large audience. The lady had them play for herself alone. The Schrammel brothers said later that during that strange concert, the doors to the adjoining room remained open. In his book "Schrammel Quartett," the author Hermann Mailer presumes that the Emperor was sitting in the nearby room to hear at least once the music that had meant so much to his son.

As we know, the Crown Prince was not only an enthusiastic listener, but also the author of lyrics for Viennese songs. Two of them have been published by Brigitte Hamann. I have before me the original manuscripts of additional songs, none of which have been published: "Das ist mein Wien," "Wiener Gfrettg'schichten," "Verschiedene Begriffe," "Na versteht si!", "Einst und Jetzt," "Ein eigener Zauber." The texts are entirely from Rudolf's pen; there can be no doubt of the authenticity of his handwriting.

The Crown Prince composed the song lyrics during the last two years of his life. Bratfisch interpreted them in his presence. After Rudolf's death, they were discovered among his papers, but no further attention was paid to them. Along with letters, manuscripts and other documents, they remained in storage in some back room of the Hofburg until the breakdown of the Monarchy. In November, 1918, before fleeing the country, Emperor Charles gave the Court official, Baron Albin Schager, papers concerning himself, his father, Archduke Otto, Emperor

---

[6] Heuriger refers to a new white wine in its first year, as often served in Viennese suburbs like Grinzing, where strolling singers, violinists and zither players often play local, popular music.

Francis Joseph and Crown Prince Rudolf.

Among the papers were the handwritten Viennese song lyrics of the deceased Prince. Dr. Schager bequeathed the papers, which at first had been taken abroad, to the Viennese Haus-, Hof-, and Staatsarchiv, where they remained after his death in December, 1941. They were there for decades before being discovered.

The historian Dr. Peter Broucek found the Schager papers while engaged in research for his book on Brigadier General Anton von Lehár, the brother of the operetta composer Franz Lehár. Broucek, who had made no use of the "treasure" told me about the song lyrics when he learned that I was writing a book on Mayerling, and I was able to obtain them through his information from the Haus-, Hof- and Staatsarchiv.[7]

---

[7] The Viennese song lyrics by Crown Prince Rudolf have been reproduced in an Appendix to this book.

The Crown Prince in Financial Difficulty
Rudolf's Friendship with Baron Hirsch

The Crown Prince's expensive lifestyle—in particular hunting excursions and affairs with women, which were his two great passions—swallowed up enormous sums of money. In contrast with other archdukes like Francis Ferdinand, who had inherited the large properties of the House of Austria-Este, or Charles, who owned the Albertina (Note: museum) and large estates, the Emperor's son had no great sources of wealth at all. He depended on his annual income of 45,000 guilders and received a monthly pay of 800 guilders as Inspector General of the Imperial infantry.[8] This was about four times as much as the salary of a university professor.

In Baron Moritz Hirsch, the Crown Prince found a really generous financier, who also became a fatherly friend. The Jewish banker was twenty-seven years older than Rudolf, came from Bavaria and lived in Paris, Brussels, London and Vienna. He had acquired extensive wealth through financing of the Balkan railway and interest in a private lottery enterprise. He helped the Crown Prince several times out of his financial difficulties.

His affairs with women represented without doubt the largest expenditures in Rudolf's private budget. One can see from the example of Mizzy Caspar how costly the love affairs were from the police records concerning the mistress: "Besides the house (Note: in Heumühlgasse), which cost 60,000 guilders, Crown Prince is reported to have given Mizi 80,000 last June. Her jewelery is worth 50,000 and was mostly purchased at Rutsky's (Mehlmarkt)." After Rudolf's death, an envelope was found in a drawer at the Hofburg addressed to Mizzy Caspar, marked "100,000 guilders," but there were only

---

[8] In 1933, 45,000 guilders = 4.5 million Austrian schillings or US$357,300.00.

30,000 in it.

Meanwhile, Marie Larisch had received the missing 70,000 guilders. She also had herself well paid for her services as an intermediary between Rudolf and Mary. The countess was heavily in debt and frequently asked Mary—the first time was right after the first meeting with the Crown Prince—to go to Rudolf, so that he could cover her "urgent debt in the amount of 25,000 guilders." Although Mary's confidante and chambermaid Agnes Jahoda advised the Baroness not to importune Rudolf with that enormous request for money, Vetsera, who was head over heels in love, felt that "she owed the countess so much for having introduced her to the Crown Prince" that she would inform Rudolf of his cousin's financial distress. Mary did this in writing and the Crown Prince sent the requested sum in a sealed envelope by a servant to the Palais Vetsera. Mary telegraphed her friend in Pardubitz and she came at once to Vienna to get the money.[9]

Like his friendship with Moriz Szeps, Rudolf's relationship with Baron Hirsch was attacked by anti-semitic groups. When the Crown Prince was recognized in September 1888 with Hirsch and the Prince of Wales, who was constantly in need of money, having breakfast together at the Hotel Imperial (this was also reported by the *Neues Wiener Tagblatt*), Rudolf was mentioned in Georg von Schönerer's newspaper *Unverfälschte Deutsche Worte*—without being named, but recognizable for everyone—as a "Judenknecht." "Whoever leads the century down the toll-road arm in arm with Baron Hirsch has to put up with malicious gossip . . . People with historical names are vying for the favor of a man with whom no honest citizen would sit at the same table."

It is incredible that, in spite of the strict censorship in the Monarchy, such attacks could get into print. Rudolf was also surprised, as he once confided to his friend Szeps on a very

---

[9] Pardubitz (Czech: Pardubice), is situated 60 mi. E of Prague, in NE Bohemia.

different occasion: "Why did this Baron Krauss (Note: Viennese Chief of Police), who has all sorts of newspapers confiscated when they write against him or Taaffe, not have it confiscated when it came out against me? It appears that I am at odds with these gentlemen. I certainly am not asking for special treatment as Crown Prince, but if they have things confiscated only to protect themselves, they should do the same when it affects me."

At the time of his death, Rudolf owed the banker Hirsch 150,000 guilders which were immediately paid by the Emperor.[10] Crown Princess Stéphanie said in her memoirs that financial concerns certainly did not cause the suicide. She added that Rudolf "had no concept of money or its value." No one ever talked about it.

---

[10] 150,000 guilders = about 15 million schillings or US $1,229,550.

A New Castle beside the Capuchin Crypt?
Flatzelsteiner at the Burgtheater

On January 16, 1992, Mr. Flatzelsteiner's crime found its way into literature. Following the tradition of Nestroy of adding up-to-date stanzas to songs, on that evening Christian Futterknecht, acting as "Schnoferl" in Nestroy's farce "Das Mädel aus der Vorstadt" (The Girl from the Suburbs) at the Theater in der Josefstadt, sang:

> Entdeckt worden ist jungst
> Ein perverser Ent-Ehrer.
> Er hat sich vergriffen
> An der Mary Vetsera.
> Einen seltsamen Gusto
> Hat Herr Flatzelsteiner.
> Für den gibt's nix Schön'res
> Als alte Gebeiner.
> Zum Gluck hab'n wir ja ein Blatt
> Im Kleinformat
> Das immer viel Sinn für d'Vergangenheit hat.
> Ja, das Ding
> Von Mayerling
> Kriegen die Leut
> Eingebleut.
> No, laßt ma an jeden sei Freud.

Three days later, on January 19th, Maria Bill included the "Flatzelsteiner Case" in her song as an "Egyptian Girl" in the première of André Heller's "Sein und Schein":

> In heißem land
> Steh' ich am Sand
> Als Pyramidenfrau.
> Doch bin ich ganz aus Österreich
> Der Trick ist alt und schlau.

Man klagt zum Beispiel,
Daß in Kairo Schreckliches passiert.
Sogar die Fürstenmumien
Werd'n dort aus dem Grab entführt.
Die Toten finden keine Ruh,
Ma braucht's als Sensation.
Mit ihre Knochen handelt man
Jetzt allerorten schon.
Der Schädel von der Potiphar
Modert in an Depot,
Das einem Möbeltandler g'hört,
Schwachsinn ist das en gros.
Wie gut, daß es solch Schändlichkeit
Nur in Ägypten gübt.
Denn gäb's sowas in Österreich,
War'n alle sehr betrübt!

The grave robbery also provided material for the cabarets. On February 1, 1993, Hans Peter Heinzl gave the following lecture on his program "Und er bewegt sich doch" at the concert house in Vienna (and a few days later on television): What is important today is in the headlines. What they have done recently was health. People have been so worried about the health of Alois Mock—and Mary Vetsera. The Crown Prince's mistress is again "in." Mayerling is more and more becoming the Austrian Loch Ness. A worldwide sensation of pressing importance. Georg Markus has finally obtained scientific proof that Mary is dead! That was not as easy as you think, because at that time the Emperor hid everything away. Vetsera's body was stored at the house of a furniture dealer in Linz and they buried half a flashlight in the grave . . . " Besides Heinzl continued, one could find this Markus, since the furniture dealer Flatzelsteiner brought him a journalistic sensation, in other furniture stores. "He is opening the drawers of all the coffers and wardrobes to see if the Crown Prince's skeleton comes to meet him."

Prior to that, Herbert Hufnagl had written in his "Kurier Kolumne" satirically in answer to a reader's question "What about the others?" on the principal question "Are the Flatzelsteiners among us?" as follows: "In order to prove that, we should have to look at all the prominent graves. Perhaps the Minister of Economics Schussel could create a Grave Opening Commission. Too bad if it proved worthwhile or did not. Then things would really get out of hand. Who emptied the graves of Beethoven, Johann Strauss or Hansi Niese? Did the specialist in the Vetsera grave robbery, Georg Markus (where is Alfred Worm?), obtain a free gift of Hans Moser on the graves black market? Is a piece of Richard Strauss stored in one of the plastic sacks of Marcel Prawy? Is Helmut Qualtinger, in one of the practical jokes he thought up when he was alive, sitting in a corner of his habitual Gutruf restaurant?"

Having in this way become a celebrity through radio, television, theatre and cabaret, Helmut Flatzelsteiner said to my colleague Christian Hauenstein at the end of January "No, I do not regret what I did. I feel that I was acting as a tool for history." Then he expressed his latest wish: the exhumation of the remains of Crown Prince Rudolf, so that the mystery of Mayerling might finally be completely cleared up.

"Herr Strudl," the satirical observer of international events for the *Kronen Zeitung*, concluded the following day: "Now Flatzelsteiner wants Crown Prince Rudolf to be exhumed. I think they ought to put a new castle beside the Capuchin crypt!"

"Then I Have Regular Cramps Again"
Rudolf's Illnesses

In the last years of his life, Rudolf was seriously ill. His body was ill, but his soul was ill too. For a long time there had been indications of the terrible end and that makes the theory of suicide the most credible of all.

The portentous constellation of his psyche was already present in the cradle. The Wittelsbachs—his mother's family—and the Habsburgs had practiced inbreeding for centuries. The wedding of Rudolf's parents was the twenty-second between the two families. Francis Joseph and Elisabeth were cousins; their marriage required a dispensation from the Pope.

In her poems, Elisabeth expressed over and again a strange yearning for death ("I died long ago"). Among the Wittelsbachs, severe psychic disturbances were not uncommon and some were even considered insane.

Rudolf was certainly not that. He was a highly intelligent person, but from a psychic standpoint, he was unstable and hypersensitive. (Of course, the opinion of the Court physician, Dr. Hermann Weiderhofer, according to which the Crown Prince had committed suicide "in a condition of mental derangement" was only issued to allow burial by the Church.)

His serious psychic problems were intensified by lifelong frustrations. Everyone recognized his depressions. A neurotic development was set in motion in early childhood by the deprivation of love, leading to the final catastrophe when the adult suffered disillusion in both his public and private lives. The Viennese expert in suicide research, Erwin Ringel, says that suicide is "not a primary reaction to difficulties and circumstances, but rather the conclusion of a behavioral pattern of the whole personality which has developed gradually and by increasing degrees." According to Professor Ringel, the cause of suicide "lies significantly more in the development of the personality and lifestyle than in the critical situation existing immediately prior to the suicide."

107

Concerning Rudolf: The origin of his voluntary death did not reside in the political and personal catastrophes of his later years, but rather in the depressive tendencies he had inherited and the neurotic pressures of his childhood.

At the beginning of 1886, the Crown Prince contracted gonorrhea, probably as a result of his commerce with women of "mixed virtue." Physical problems were now added to the psychic ones. At that time it was customary to try to alleviate the venereal infections with mercury. During this sexual illness, Rudolf suffered inflammation of the urethra and the connective membranes of his eyes. He had pain in his joints. Whereas today the illness could have been cured within a few days, a hundred years ago the physicians were powerless against it.

Crown Prince Rudolf tried to rid himself of depression and physical infirmities with alcohol and drugs. But the fateful mixture of champagne and cognac with morphine and cocaine, the latter originally recommended by doctors to relieve his suffering, led to stomach cramps and asthmatic type attacks of coughing. In March, 1887, he wrote to his wife Stéphanie, "I cannot get rid of my coughing. It often stops for several hours and then I have regular cramps again . . . I am fighting it with morphine, which is harmful in itself."

"This information clearly proves that Rudolf was taking morphine," wrote Hans Bankl in his book *How They Really Died*. "It has been proven beyond a doubt that the Crown Prince was addicted two years before his death. Rudolf gave himself subcutaneous injections, but it appears that he also tried to break off the habit. Those close to him were aware of the symptoms of withdrawal. His use of morphine, alcohol and women during the stages of depression hastened his physical decline."

Rudolf lost weight, became prematurely old, and was plagued with gastritis, permanent headaches and severe insomnia. In general, he only slept for four hours. Suffering officially from "rheumatic conditions," he infected his wife with the venereal disease during a joint holiday on the Dalmatian island of Lacroma. "I was only able to enjoy that magnificent excursion for a few days," Stéphanie wrote in her memoirs, "then I became seriously ill. I lay for weeks in bed with indescribable pain. Professors from Vienna and Trieste said that I had peritonitis. I did not suspect the reason for my illness. Everything was kept quiet and the doctors were sworn to secrecy. It was only later that I discovered and learned that the Crown Prince was responsible for my illness. He too had fallen victim to the frightful disease which spares no one, whether of low degree or the level of the throne, whenever their thoughtlessness or execrable heritage opens the door . . ."

Stéphanie's Fallopian tubes had been inflamed by the venereal disease, leading to sterility in the Crown Princess. The couple did indeed have a daughter, Archduchess Elisabeth, born in 1883, but their hope for a masculine successor to the throne was now buried. That was a grievous blow for Rudolf and his wife.

In the summer of 1886, Rudolf's tendency towards self destruction became evident. The twenty-eight-year-old wrote in his diary: "From time to time I seek an opportunity to see someone who is dying and to listen to his last breath. For me, this is always a remarkable sight and of all the people whom I have seen dying, each one has died in a different way. I am also trying to accustom my wife to this sight. One has to learn to deal with the final needs.

Suddenly, Rudolf began to express dark premonitions of death. He read stories of suicide and said, whenever people discussed the future of the monarchy: "You will see that I shall not be there!" He referred to his future suicide, in a hidden way, to Archdukes Francis Ferdinand, Otto and Frederick, as well as to the Duke of Braganza and the painter Franz von Pausinger—without any of those gentlemen taking it seriously. According to Professor Bankl, Rudolf gave evidence in the last two and a half years of his life of all the symptoms which are considered in modern psychiatry as early stages of suicide:

1. Personal isolation and a growing feeling of having no way out; depressions and helpless fear of a future which he

considered with pessimism.

2. Violent, but powerless, attacks on the system of government and its highest representative, his father. Out of this came resignation and feelings of guilt.

3. Flight into a world of fantasy with thoughts and conversations about death.

At that time Rudolf asked the anatomist Emil Zuckerkandl, the son-in-law of his friend Moriz Szeps, "if it was not eerie to live at the Anatomical Institute, surrounded by corpses and skeletons, in an atmosphere of death."

"No, even the skulls of the dead have a certain beauty," replied the Professor, "and soon people will accept the idea that death is not a misfortune, but rather a necessary, wondrous fulfillment of life." In that way it is possible that the celebrated doctor strengthened the Crown Prince in the decision he had made long before to want to die. In any case, he asked Zuckerkandl to give him a skull. During the last weeks of his life, Rudolf had it lying on his desk in the Hofburg beside a revolver. His death-wish could not have been more clearly expressed to those closest to him than by that macabre scene.

Even Mary Vetsera came into contact with the death's head. "I explored everything," she wrote to her friend Hermine Tobis after her first visit to Rudolf at the Hofburg. "A revolver and a death's head lay on the desk. I took up the latter and looked at it from every side. Suddenly, he entered (Note: Rudolf) and with great alarm took it from me. When I told him that I was not at all afraid, he smiled."

Contemporaries have confirmed that Rudolf's public addresses, which had once been brilliant, were becoming increasingly meaningless; that very little remained of his scientific and literary qualities; that he changed his ideas and political outlook in a disconnected manner. Numerous rumors were already flying through the monarchy to the effect that these derangements stemmed from an ear infection allegedly inherited from the Wittelsbachs, or resulting from a fall from a horse.

110

On March 1, 1887, Crown Prince Rudolf drew up his last will and testament. "I have written this following testament in my own hand and in full possession of all my faculties and dutifully ask His Imperial, Royal and Apostolic Majesty to accept the burden of Testament-Executor, and also to take over the guardianship of my daughter Elisabeth. I name my daughter Elisabeth as sole heir to my movable and immovable property; I name my wife Stéphanie to have lifelong usufruct of all the property. In case of her remarriage, the usufruct ceases entirely and passes to my daughter. If my daughter marries, the usufruct will be divided between both."

A few days after he had drawn up his testament, Crown Princess Stéphanie found her husband "deeply changed. Not only that his health was threatened, but his insomnia had increased; his passion for hunting had grown to extreme limits and he spent his evenings with groups to which I could not follow. I felt clearly that he had slipped away from me entirely, drawn down into another world. Today we know that the Crown Prince's changed conduct was only the result of the severe moral and political conflict from which he could not liberate himself. It was a time which was decisive for the destiny of Crown Prince Rudolf . . . It was sad that while all of this was brewing, no one knew anything about it or did not want to know. Later it happened that the Crown Prince did not return home till early in the morning in an unpleasant condition. In such a situation, it was no longer possible for us to have a real common life; my whole being rebelled against it."

Nevertheless, Stéphanie must be credited with the fact that she was the only family member who recognized the threatening situation of the Crown Prince and tried to save him. Upon her return from a Mediterranean cruise in January, 1889, she was so frightened at Rudolf's appearance that she decided to speak with the Emperor in order frankly to open his eyes to his son's condition.

"I clung to the idea that his intervention would help and save us," she recalled. "Although it was not permitted to see the Emperor without being announced, I gathered up my courage and had my name taken in immediately by a chamberlain. The Emperor received me with cordiality. I started off by saying that Rudolf was very ill and that his appearance and actions were causing me grave concern; I asked him earnestly to send his son soon on an extended tour of the world to get him away from his destructive way of life. Then the Emperor interrupted me: 'That is your imagination. Rudolf lacks nothing. He only looks pale. He is too much on the go. He tries to do too much. He ought to stay more with you. Don't be worried!' The Emperor embraced me; I kissed his hand. I was dismissed and everything I had wanted to tell the Emperor remained unsaid. I staggered into the anteroom and had to hold on to an armchair. Was that all I had left from my last hope? It seemed to me that the Crown Prince's fate was sealed. I feared the worst: A slow decay, more terrible than death."

Despite many visible signs, the Emperor had not understood the critical danger threatening his only son or did not want to understand it. His daughter-in-law was not even allowed to speak to him about it.

It was probably a result of his great isolation in his childhood—his mother constantly traveling, his father only interested in the administration of the Empire—that Rudolf was unable to be alone even in his adult years. Just as he was afraid of living alone, he was also probably afraid of dying alone. So it became his ardent desire to die with another person.

It was the fate of Mary Vetsera to be the "chosen one" in this insane plan.

"Not Deserve to Be My Successor"
The Road to Mayerling

The decision for suicide must have been made on January 26, 1889. At nine o'clock in the morning, Rudolf had an audience with the Emperor, during which a frightful dispute arose. Of course there were no witnesses to that argument, but several interpretations as to what occurred during that conversation between father and son at the Hofburg.

Version 1: Rudolf asked his father's consent to requesting that the Pope annul his marriage to Crown Princess Stéphanie.

Version 2: Rudolf was a member of the Freemasons, and the Emperor asked him to account for his membership in that secret association which was forbidden in Austria at that time. It is certain that the Crown Prince supported the Freemasons and their liberal, antiracist and anticlerical ideology, but up to now there has been no irrefutable evidence that he was truly a member of a lodge.

Version 3: Emperor Francis Joseph asked his son to break off his relationship with Mary Vetsera, of which he had become aware. This is indicated in a farewell letter to her sister Hanna, which was discovered later in one of Mary's dresses (the original of which is not at hand): "Today he finally made clear to me the impossibility that I could be his; he gave his father his word of honor to leave me. It is finished! I am going to die happily."

Version 4: It had seeped through that Baroness Vetsera is expecting a child from the successor to the throne. This version is supported by the "previously mentioned police report, confirming her four-month pregnancy. Hence the awful scene between father and son on the 20th of this month."

Version 5: Complete disagreement between father and son on Austro-Hungarian foreign policy. It had to be decided during the year which had just begun whether the Dual Alliance with Germany should be extended. Whereas Rudolf spoke openly against it, for Francis Joseph there was no alternative.

A letter supporting this "political version" was found in Rudolf's room a few hours after his death by the head criminal investigator (and later Chief of Police) Baron Ferdinand Gorup, who copied it, as he thought it important for historical reasons: "Farewell! Time is pressing. I conclude: the Emperor will not abdicate in the foreseeable future. He is steering towards destruction. Endless waiting amidst profoundly vexatious and often serious conflicts is unbearable." Like many other Mayerling papers, the original of this handwritten letter by Rudolf has disappeared.

Whichever of the five versions is correct, it is quite possible, even probable, that several circumstances led simultaneously to the catastrophe At the end of the audience, when the door to the antechamber was already open, the Emperor said the famous words to Rudolf, which Francis Joseph's chamberlain Beck claims to have heard: "You do not deserve to be my successor!" Other members of the staff observed that when the Crown Prince left the Imperial apartment "he seemed to be frightfully upset, plainly crushed and was visibly trembling."

Still, on that Saturday, Rudolf went on as usual. After the audience, he sat at his desk in the Franz Josef-Kaserne, disposed of his correspondence and held various conferences. He even occupied himself with an ornithological study of a rare forest bird, which proves that he was intellectually active right to the end.

On that day Rudolf was thinking positively of the future, sending the following letter to Josef von Weilen, editor of the German-language edition of the *Kronprinzenwerk*, for which he was working on an essay concerning the Imperial hunting lodge Gödöllö, north of Budapest: "Dear Weilen! It has not been possible for me to write the sketch on Gödöllö up to now. As you know, I have been overwhelmed with a lot of military work and now I have to go through the qualification lists, which has to be done carefully and takes much time. But when I get to Mayerling on Monday I shall find a few hours of rest to complete the essay on Gödöllö . . . I hope to see you on

Wednesday or Thursday and give you the manuscript then. Sincerely, Your Rudolf."

The Crown Prince could not have left us better proof of his desire to live, which was still present, at least from time to time, on that day. However, it seems clear that the discussion with the Emperor was decisive in his determination to end his life.

In the late afternoon, Mary called on her confidante Marie Larisch in Room 21 at the Grand Hotel. "She was pale as a ghost," the countess recalled later, "and her eyes seemed too large for her face. I had the impression that something awful had befallen her." Apparently her mother had become alarmed by the affair of the cigarette case and wanted to put Mary into a cloister. After Mary's visit in the hotel Larisch drove Mary to her home where, according to Helene Vetsera, she suffered "a kind of nervous attack" and went to bed early.

Sunday, January 27, 1889. Preparations were made for the suicide. The Crown Prince informed his brother-in-law Philip Coburg—married to Stéphanie's elder sister Louise—and his friend Joseph Hoyos that the hunt which had been planned at Mayerling, after being advanced by a few days, would begin on Tuesday.

The Crown Prince gave his cousin Marie Larisch a locked casket, telling her "that only one person knows the secret and besides me he alone has the right to ask its return . . . His name is not important. You can give it to the individual who mentions four signs to you. Write them down and repeat them." Rudolf dictated the letters "R.I.O.U." (Mayerling specialists believe that the use of initials which is typical of Freemasons gives further proof that the Crown Prince was the member of a lodge. The letters could mean "Respectable, Inner Orient, Hungary." Marie Larisch states in her memoirs that she later gave the casket to Archduke Johann Salvator (Johann Orth) who, according to that, must have known the prince's secret.

Mary asked Countess Larisch to promise to bring her the following morning secretly to Rudolf in the Hofburg. The little

Baroness already knew that she "was allowed" to follow him to Mayerling—and also to death. Helene Vetsera wrote that this prospect made her on that day "wildly happy."

In the evening, the Crown Prince took part in a reception for the German ambassador Prince Heinrich Reuss against his will, but at his father's express command. The reception was given in honor of Emperor Wilhelm's birthday. One of the guests, the architect Freiherr Friedrich von Schmidt, was impressed by the variations which were typical of Rudolf's unstable psyche: "He joined groups and spoke with three or four persons in his always friendly way. When he turned away to look for another place, he was changed, almost flaccid, with a vacant look, as though he had taken off his former manner."

One of the persons with whom Rudolf spoke "in his enormously friendly manner" was the celebrated surgeon, Theodor Billroth, at whose instance the Crown Prince had assumed patronage ten years before of the "Rudolfinerverein" (Note: Rudolf Society), named for him. The society had been established in order to bring about improvement in patient care, which was urgently needed. A nursing school for women, free of ecclesiastical oversight, and the Rudolfiner House, were opened, in spite of strong opposition by clerical groups. Now, at the German ambassador's reception, Rudolf approached Billroth "and talked to me at unusual length. He was friendly and warm with me as he had been on the day of our first meeting in Prague (Note: 1879) at Hradcany Castle. He was always like that wherever I met him, as recently at Abbazia during the Christmas holidays, where we strolled along, chatting together without formality."[11] It was apparent that the physician did not perceive any change in the psyche of the Crown Prince on that evening.

---

[11] Abbazia = Opatija, a town in NW Croatia, 7 mi. W of Rijeka (Ital.: Fiume). A popular winter and summer resort. Sea bathing.

Rudolf's wife Stéphanie also came to the German embassy and Mary Vetsera took part in the reception too. Rudolf's aide-de-camp Freiherr Giesl von Gieslingen stated later: "I remember how impressed I was by the striking beauty of Baroness Mary. She was slender, of medium height, with beautifully seductive features, fascinating, large blue eyes with long black lashes, full black hair that stood like a crown on her head and on it a crescent with large, shining diamonds. I cannot say whether the Crown Prince spoke with the Baroness that evening, as I was on duty then and constantly observed the Crown Prince. I noted an unusually large group around Professor Tilgner (Note: the sculptor Viktor Tilgner). Only later did I learn that Baroness Vetsera was sitting behind Professor Tilgner . . . "

After the soirée, Rudolf went to the Hofburg, where he called for Moriz Szeps, who found him "prodigiously agitated." "The Emperor has dishonored and insulted me in public," the Crown Prince told his political friend. "Now all bonds between him and me are broken. Now I feel that I am free!"

Brigitte Hamann assumes that the ceremony at the embassy, "being a demonstration in favor of the German-Austrian alliance," must have driven him to despair just as much as his personal problems. "This was a preparation for the extension of the Dual Alliance which was planned for October, 1889, against which Rudolf was so desperately struggling. If annulment and remarriage had really been the main problem in those days, Rudolf would scarcely have had cause to call Szeps that night after the reception."

Following his conversation with Szeps, the Crown Prince had himself driven to Mizzy Caspar in Heumühlgasse, where he spent several hours that night. The authorities knew about it, for the police agent, Dr. Florian Meissner, who had been observing the house on the Wieden for weeks, reported to the Chief of Police: "On Monday, January 28, 1889, E.R. (Note: Archduke Rudolf) with Mizi until three o'clock in the morning. He drank a lot of champagne and gave the house porter ten guilders for letting him in and out. When he left Mizi, contrary to his custom, he made the sign of the cross on her forehead. From Mizi he drove (direct?) to Mayerling."

In this, the otherwise conscientious agent was mistaken. Rudolf was not going to Mayerling yet and certainly not at all "directly." First, he went to his apartment in the Hofburg, where he tried to sleep for a few hours.

Monday, January 28, 1889, Hofburg. After finishing his daily routine work, Rudolf sat down at his desk to write several letters of farewell. He wrote to his sister, Marie Valerie, Baron Moritz Hirsch, Mizzy Caspar and Crown Princess Stéphanie: "You are free of my presence and vexation," he wrote his wife, "be happy in your own way. Be good to the poor little girl, who is all that remains of me. Give my last greetings to all our acquaintances, especially Bombelles, Spindler, Latour, Wowo, Gisela, Leopold, etc., etc.—I am going to die calmly. This alone can save my good name. Embracing you affectionately, Your loving Rudolf."

The letter to Stéphanie is the only one of which the original has been preserved. Brigitte Hamann is convinced that the casket which is being withheld by the Habsburg family contains the crime weapon ("from which two rounds are missing"), Mary's handkerchief and also Rudolf's farewell letters to Mizzy Caspar and Baron Hirsch and the note to the valet Loschek. Possibly also the letter to Marie Larisch and some material concerning Bratfisch's testimony to the police.

The Crown Prince addressed another letter in Hungarian to Count Ladislaus Szögyenyi-Marich, section head in the Imperial Foreign Ministry. "I must die. It is the only way to leave this world at least as a gentleman. Be so kind as to open the desk here in Vienna in the Turkish Room where, in better times, we so often sat together, and deal with the papers as written in my last will, which is enclosed herewith. With sincere greetings and with all good wishes for our adored Hungarian Fatherland, I am your faithful Rudolf."

This letter, clearly written in Vienna, is considered by historians as another proof of Rudolf's decision to die prior to his departure for Mayerling. This eliminates any other version than that of double suicide. It also excludes that of a failed abortion.

Marie Larisch stormed into Baron Krauss' office at about noon on January 28th, in order "to inform him discreetly" that she was in the city during the morning with Baroness Vetsera. When the countess got out of the fiacre for a moment at the Kohlmarkt, Mary was supposed to wait for her. But when Larisch returned, Vetsera had disappeared. We learn from the Chief of Police memorandum for the record that "the countess found a note in the fiacre in which the baroness expressed in a few words her intention to take her own life."

What the countess did not tell the police chief was that she had called for Mary at 10 A.M. at the Palais Vetsera in the Salesianergasse to bring her—not to the Kohlmarkt—but directly to Rudolf at the Hofburg. Mary left her there and got into the fiacre of the Prince's own coachman Bratfisch and departed with him in the direction of Mayerling. The note that she really left behind for Larisch read as follows: "I cannot live any longer. Today I have a head start. When you catch up with me, I shall be directly in the Danube." Later, the investigative commission found on Rudolf's desk in the Hofburg these words scratched onto an ashtray by Mary with an ink pen: "Better revolver, not poison. Revolver is more certain."

Mary's mother referred to Marie Larisch's calling for her daughter—and not without reason—as flight from her parents' home, for which the countess gave her full support. In fact, Larisch's rôle in the entire Mayerling affair is more than shadowy. Even if she now tried to prevent the worst by going to the Chief of Police, she cannot be absolved of a considerable portion of guilt. It was she who encouraged the naïve desire of the little baroness which surely could not have a happy ending. She encouraged her and helped her to turn her romantic "crush" into fact. And Marie Larisch did not even do that for honest reasons, but rather, as we know, for a lot of money.

While the countess was speaking with the chief of police, Mary was on her way to Breitenfurt, where she was to meet

Rudolf. The Crown Prince left the Hofburg towards twelve o'clock in a one-horse carriage. The coachman, who returned the vehicle to Vienna later, sat on the back seat. Rudolf urged the Lippizan towards Breitenfurt at a gallop. The secret policemen who were following him noted that for that distance of seventeen km, he only required one and a half hours. As agreed, he met Mary and Bratfisch at the resort restaurant "Roter Stadl," about half way to Mayerling. Bratfisch drove them both to the hunting lodge. They arrived there, having made a detour, as darkness set in. The secret police did not follow him that far. They chose to turn back shortly before reaching their goal.

One must bear in mind that nearly forty hours went by from the time of Marie Larisch's urgent plea to the Chief of Police until the deed was carried out, without the police being able to interfere. And this, even though they were aware of the relationship between Mary and Rudolf. And even though they knew that both the Crown Prince and his mistress intended to die.

Marie Larisch surmised that Mary and Rudolf were on their way to Mayerling and spontaneously suggested to the Chief of Police to have the Crown Prince's hunting lodge placed under observation. Krauss knew no other way out of it than to excuse himself through the bureaucracy. "I could only say that Mayerling lay outside the police area and that I was not able to deal with it officially or to inquire into it and that even in Vienna I had no authority to make inquiry at the Burg. The police have nothing to do with the Court building at Mayerling."

But it would not have been prohibited for the Chief of Police to report to the Emperor's chancellery that the Crown Prince and his mistress were in grave danger.

Meanwhile, the momentous events continued on their dramatic course.

Mayerling Castle is located on a small hill in the southern Vienna Woods. Formerly there had been a cloister in the main building. The Crown Prince had purchased it two years earlier and rebuilt it as a private residence. It was filled with trophies and a lot of pictures, mostly of hunting scenes. Rudolf loved the little castle above everything, although—or perhaps because—it had a melancholy atmosphere.

On the following morning, January 29, 1889, Count Hoyos and Prince Coburg met there at 8:10 A.M. Hoyos: "After about five or ten minutes the Crown Prince appeared in morning dress, sat down with us to breakfast and wished us a hearty good morning. He related that his carriage (Note: on the way to Mayerling) could only be brought over the slippery, icy mountain beside Gaaden with a pair of farmer's horses. He, without taking off his fur, had helped to push the vehicle, had run and caught a cold . . . " The Crown Prince did not say a word of having come to Mayerling with Baroness Vetsera. Only Bratfisch and Loschek knew of her presence.

Apparently because of his cold, Rudolf did not take part in the hunt on that day. Whereas Prince Coburg returned to Vienna after a relatively short deer-stalking, in order to follow the Emperor's invitation to a family dinner, Hoyos remained at Mayerling. "I returned from the hunt at about 5:30 to my apartment which is about five hundred steps from the little Mayerling Castle (in the former workshop) and was asked to dine at 7 o'clock. After a while, the Crown Prince came into the billiard room (ground floor right from the entrance), where I waited and where we were to dine . . . "

Meanwhile, Prince Coburg, coming from Mayerling, came to the family dinner, at which Crown Prince Rudolf was also expected to participate. After all, it was being given to celebrate the engagement of his sister Marie Valerie to Archduke Francis Salvator. Stéphanie, for whom it was obviously painful to sit at that event which was important for the family, recalls: "When I entered to hall, it seemed as though all eyes were directed towards me. The Emperor and Empress asked me where Rudolf was. I replied that he had caught cold and wanted to take care of himself. He had been ill for quite a while and I was worried about the way he looked. However, I did not dare to express my fears as far as to ask that a doctor be sent to Mayerling." After the dinner, the Crown Princess, with her sister-in-law Marie Valerie and her bridegroom went to a show at the Renz Circus in Vienna.

Meanwhile, according to Hoyos, during his evening meal with Rudolf at Mayerling, they only talked about inconsequential things. "The Crown Prince asked about the results of the hunt and other matters. He mentioned that tomorrow's hunt at Schöpflgitter promised greater success and then he sat down to dinner, where I was the only guest." While Rudolf and Hoyos enjoyed roast venison and dessert at their elegantly laid table, Mary spent the time of the two-hour dinner alone in the Crown Prince's bedroom-cum-study.

Hoyos continued: "After we had smoked and it came to nine o'clock, the Crown Prince withdrew, saying that he had to take care of his cold, all this with his usual cordiality."

"I had not the slightest notion," added Count Hoyos, "that I had shaken that hand for the last time!"

Joseph Hoyos went to the hunting lodge's guest house, which was off to one side and went to bed at ten o'clock.

Rudolf and Mary had Bratfisch sing a few more songs for them and play the bagpipe. Reportedly, the prince's coachman sang the Crown Prince's favorite song "Der Schwalbe Gruss" three times. Then they remained alone in the bedroom to write additional letters of farewell. Rudolf to the Empress: (this letter has disappeared, but Elisabeth's lady-in-waiting Ida von Ferenczy left its content for us. Surprisingly, the Crown Prince repeated in it almost verbatim what the Emperor had said to him during their last private interview. He wrote: "I know very well that I did not deserve to be his son."

Among Mary's farewell letters was one to her sister Hanna: "We are both going happily into the unknown beyond. Think of me from time to time, be happy and marry only for love. I was unable to do it and since I could not resist love, I am going with him. Your Mary. Do not cry for me. I am going to the other side in peace. It is beautiful out here. Once more: Good-bye."

She wrote the following words to her mother: "Pardon me

for what I have done. I could not resist love. In agreement with him, I want to be buried beside him in the cemetery of Alland. I am happier in death than in life. Your Mary."

And there is a postscript symptomatic of the unfathomable in Viennese life, the established proximity of laughter and tears, of the joy of living and yearning for death: The seventeen-year-old girl left as her final words to her closest relatives before she died: "Bratfisch played the pipes wonderfully."

The Valet's Viewing of the Dead
January 30, 1889

Prince Coburg was expected to return to Mayerling on that dismally-cold Wednesday of January 30, 1889, shortly after eight o'clock on the train from Vienna. Afterwards, as the Crown Prince had proposed the previous evening, the three gentlemen intended to have breakfast together. Count Hoyos wrote: "It was only a few minutes before that time, and I was quite ready, when my valet announced the castle warder Zwerger. When the latter came in, he told me that Loschek wanted me to know that His Imperial Highness the Crown Prince could not be awakened. When I replied that he must have slept well and soundly, he gave further information to the effect that the Crown Prince had been up at 6:30, had gone into the anteroom in his dressing gown and given Loschek, who was in the neighboring room, instructions to awaken him again at 7:30 and to order breakfast and the coachman Bratfisch for the same time with his carriage; then, whistling, he returned to his bedroom. Loschek had been knocking now since 7:30, first with his finger and then with a stick of firewood, on the bedroom door, but no sign of life occurred. He said the bedroom door to the antechamber was locked, as well as the door leading from the spiral staircase of the first floor to the sleeping quarters, which was also locked and the keys were there."

Suspecting something serious, Hoyos followed Zwerger to the main building, where Loschek confirmed what the castle warder had said. The count knocked several times and called out loudly to Rudolf. "Since Loschek did not want to take responsibility for breaking in the door, I gave the order to break open the door immediately on my responsibility," reported Joseph Hoyos. "Only then did Loschek say that the Crown Prince was not alone and added that there was a Baroness Vetsera with him."

This information caused Hoyos "the greatest consternation,

all the more so as I had no idea of the baroness' presence at Mayerling nor even of relations between her and the Crown Prince and for me there was not the smallest reason to assume any relations, even distant ones." (At least, the last half sentence from Hoyos's pen, from an intimate friend of the Crown Prince, is not very credible. The count cannot have been unaware that Rudolf enjoyed the reputation of being a ladies' man.)

At that moment, Prince Coburg arrived at Mayerling, coming from the railway station in a fiacre. Hoyos apprised him of the situation, "and, after talking it over for a few minutes, we decided to have the door broken open on our responsibility." Loschek was to carry this out.

After the valet had opened the room with force and glanced within, he told Hoyos and Coburg that the lovers were dead, the Crown Prince was lying "bent over the edge of the bed with a large pool of blood in front of him, presumably poisoned with potassium cyanide, since that kind of hemorrhage happens then."

A really amateurish "viewing of the dead" by the valet, which was to be the source of much confusion.

After a short conference, the two aristocrats agreed that Hoyos should undertake the task of notifying the Emperor of this inconceivable event, since Rudolf's brother-in-law Coburg "crushed by pain was hardly able to take any action". Hoyos asked the Court physician Dr. Widerhofer to come to Mayerling at once, without giving any reason in his telegram, and then drove with Bratfisch to the nearby railway station at Baden.

Meanwhile the criminal investigators which had finally been dispatched by the Chief of Police Krauss arrived at Mayerling and all they could do was to confirm the death of the two. Commissioner Baron Ferdinand Gorup, who arrived later, described the atmosphere at Mayerling as follows: "Mayerling was surrounded by a cordon of gendarmerie and a mass of police officers encircled the hunting castle. However, I looked in vain for any officials in the castle; besides the warder

Zwerger, there was no living soul on hand. A sinister silence lay over the rooms. One could not find any member of the Court, any government official or any of the gentlemen who otherwise lived in the castle."

Count Hoyos had the express train from Trieste which came at 9:18 stopped by the stationmaster, saying that the Crown Prince had committed suicide. Then he went on to Vienna. At 10:11 Hoyos entered the Swiss Court at the Hofburg to inform Rudolf's chamberlain, Count Carl Bombelles, and the Emperor's aide-de-camp, Count Eduard Paar, of the catastrophe. Paar felt that he was unable to give that news to Francis Joseph. "For me, it is impossible. A thing of this kind can only be said by Her Majesty."

So the gentlemen hurried over to the Empress, who was just having a Greek lesson. Elisabeth broke down in tears. When she regained control of herself, her first reaction was: "How can we inform the Emperor of this frightful blow of fate?"

Elisabeth went quickly to the room of her lady-in-waiting, Ida Ferenczy. Francis Joseph arrived a few minutes later, for he knew that his soul-sister Katharina Schratt was there. It was she, the actress, who found the courage after a short time to break the silence. "Majesty, the Crown Prince is . . . very ill."

The Emperor could not believe the words. The attitude of the others present was only too clear. "Is he dead?" he asked. Elisabeth nodded. "Yes, he is dead."

Francis Joseph hid his face in his hands and murmured several times to himself: "This is terrible!"

Then Count Hoyos—apparently on the basis of the erroneous assumption of the valet Loschek—told the Emperor that his son had been poisoned by a girl named Mary Vetsera. It was also reported to Baroness Helene Vetsera that her daughter had killed the Crown Prince.

It seems as though people in the Imperial government thought for a long time of making the version that Mary had murdered Rudolf official.

Helene Vetsera tells us in her memoirs that a highly placed

individual informed her "that they had eaten breakfast together and it is presumed that she poisoned him and then herself at that time." Mary's mother defended herself desperately against that cold, made-up plan of Count Taaffe to characterize the baroness, who had been shot to death, as the murderer of the unsuspecting prince. This version finally had to be dropped because of the conscientious attitude of the Imperial house physician, Dr. Widerhofer, who did not allow himself to be coerced into making a false death certificate.

Towards evening, Hoyos called on Crown Princess Stéphanie, who remarked during the audience "that she had seen this misfortune coming."

Not until the following morning did Hofrat Dr. Hermann Widerhofer make his report to the king. "Tell me everything," commanded Francis Joseph. "I want to know everything exactly as it is."

As for the doctor, he thought that his Imperial master had already been informed of the details of what happened at Mayerling and began with a consolation. "I can assure Your Majesty that His Imperial Highness did not suffer for a moment. The shot went directly into the head."

Then the monarch, who was otherwise self-controlled, became angry. "What is this you are saying about a shot?"

"Yes, Majesty. The bullet with which he shot himself," replied the physician.

"He shot himself? That is not true. She poisoned him! Rudolf shot himself. You have to be able to prove what you are saying."

Shaken by the paternal grief, Dr. Widerhofer then had to report how the facts at the site of the tragedy—the careful laying out of the body of the baroness, the manner of the shot which was made in front of a mirror placed on the night table for greater accuracy—ruled out any doubt that the Crown Prince had turned the weapon against himself. The Emperor broke down for a moment and wept "in even greater pain".[12]

---

[12] This description was taken from the diary of Archduchess Marie Valerie, Rudolf's younger sister.

"Everything Disposed Of, Habrda"
The Fate of Certain Persons after Mayerling

The news of the catastrophe seeped as early as the afternoon of January 30th into the farthest corners of Austria-Hungary, and black flags were raised over all public buildings. Fifty million subjects of the multinational country, no matter the nationality, race or religion to which they belonged, were paralyzed. It was not only that one of the most popular men in the Monarchy had died: but the death of the Crown Prince was also connected to a crime such as had never before been experienced "in those circles." Eduard Hanslick wrote in his memoirs: "The bleak, hopeless excitement that affected the whole population was indescribable. I have lived through the saddest catastrophes in Vienna: revolutions, unsuccessful military campaigns, lost provinces, fatal devastations from water and fire, but none of all that could be compared to this horrible January 30th."

Although nothing was said at first in our country of the true extent of the tragedy and the death of Mary Vetsera, the first rumors soon began to circulate. Foreign newspapers were smuggled in, which depended of course on speculation alone, since the official authorities maintained an ironclad silence. In this way, dozens of fanciful Mayerling legends arose throughout the world and by its awkward conduct the Court itself constantly added to the gossip.

The dead Crown Prince was removed from the hunting lodge in a hearse and taken to Vienna by rail. Rudolf's aide-de-camp, Arthur Giesl von Gieslingen, who acted as honor guard at the deathbed where the Crown Prince lay in his bedroom at the Hofburg, recalled that on the first day he had to tell all visitors that Rudolf had died of a heart attack. "I and those who were close by had to cling to what Prince Hohenlohe had told us. It was not an easy task. During the morning there came many members of the royal family, ladies and gentlemen from the various sections of the Court, ministers and men who were close to the Crown Prince, including Count Stefan Karolyi who had often been with the deceased at Laxenburg and the Hofburg. All were told that the cause of death had been a heart attack. Count Karolyi was suspicious of that and asked me for details, why there was a bandage on the head, etc. I answered that the Crown Prince had injured himself on the head when he fell from the bed at the time of the attack. My reply was not credible, but I could not think of a better one."

On February 2, 1889, the *Wiener Zeitung* finally published the results of the post mortem examination after Rudolf's body had been examined at the Hofburg by Professor Hans Kundrat, head of the Pathological-Anatomical Institute in Vienna, Eduard von Hofmann, a forensic doctor, and Hermann Widerhofer, the Imperial court physician. Two days went by between the examination and the publication of the results, because Rudolf's principal tutor, Count Carl Bombelles, placed the doctors under heavy pressure to decide on "death through cardiac arrest," which had been announced at first. The highly reputable physicians rejected that demand and threatened to resign if the Court continued to insist on it.

Their expert opinion concluded:

1. His Imperial Highness died chiefly from shattering of the skull and the anterior portion of the brain.
2. This shattering was caused by a shot fired directly against the area of the right front temple.
3. A shot from a revolver of medium caliber was capable of causing an injury such as that described above.
4. The projectile was not present, as it emerged through the exit opening observed above the left ear.
5. There is no doubt that His Imperial Highness fired the shot himself and that death occurred instantaneously.

It was only at number six that the doctors were willing to compromise, accepting the request of the Court to the effect that, on the basis of defective growth and other abnormalities in the cranium, it might be assumed "that the act took place in a condition of mental derangement." It was only the addition of this paragraph which allowed ecclesiastical blessing of the corpse.

Hundreds of wreaths and countless chrysanthemums, orchids, roses and carnations, which had to be brought during that cold winter season from hothouses, formed a gigantic sea of flowers as a bed for the body which lay in state at the Hofburg.

On the two days prior to the interment, the population had an opportunity to take leave of the dead Crown Prince. More than 100,000 people came to the court chapel, but due to lack of time and space only 30,000 were able to get in. The Viennese recalled an old prophecy according to which the Habsburg dynasty which had begun with Rudolf I, who founded the Austrian house in the thirteenth century, would end with a Habsburg, likewise named Rudolf. Rudolf found his last resting place in the Capuchin Crypt on February 5th. The Emperor collapsed beside his son's coffin and had to be assisted until he regained control of himself. The interment was then made with all the splendor provided for in the Spanish court ritual in the case of the death of an archduke.

On the contrary, Baroness Vetsera's last road could not have been more undignified. On the evening of January 31, 1889, huddled in coat, hat and veil, Mary's mortal remains were forced into a fiacre, because a second hearse would have aroused suspicion among the population. A broom handle was tied to the back to hold the lifeless body upright so that curious persons along the highway would not gain the impression that a dead person was being removed from the Crown Prince's hunting lodge. Her uncles Alexander Baltazzi and Count Georg Stockau sat on Mary's left and right and there was a police commissioner beside the coachman. This strange party passed through a dirty, cold, wintry landscape, over icy, snow-covered roads, to the nearby Cistercian monastery at Heiligenkreuz, in whose cemetery the body was to be secretly buried.

As the consecrated ground was frozen, the gravediggers who had been quickly assembled were unable to excavate the grave on time, so that the interment could not take place before the morning of February 1st, in extreme secrecy. In order to avoid attracting attention, not even Mary's mother was permitted to take part in the event. Besides a few monks and the two uncles of the deceased, there were three policemen present. Among them was Chief Commissioner Johann Habrda, who sent the following message to Chief of Police Krauss after the ceremony: "Telegram from Heiligenkreuz to Chief of Police, Vienna, dated 1.2.1889. Everything disposed of, Habrda."

"Everything disposed of, Habrda." It would not have been possible to say more cold-bloodedly how the plan for hiding the dead Vetsera worked out by Prime Minister Taaffe and Chief of Police Krauss was carried out. Court Secretary Dr. Heinrich von Slatin, who was responsible for the "orderly execution" of the irreverent interment wrote in his memoirs: "I knew that carrying out this order was contrary to lawful regulations." It was also Slatin who, together with the house physician Dr. Auchenthaler, "had to confirm Mary's suicide, because otherwise her immediate burial would not have been possible under the law. We both did this on our own responsibility, which was generally approved."

Dr. Slatin answered the early protests of Mary's uncles Baltazzi and Stockau, saying: "It had to be stated in the records that this was a suicide, because otherwise there would have had to be a report to the courts and then there would have had to be a court-ordered investigation, which would have attracted a lot of attention." After an investigation by the criminal police, it would not have been possible to sustain the allegation of Mary's "suicide".

But who could investigate this case, if the Emperor's son was the only possible culprit?

There were many human tragedies resulting from this

drama. Rudolf and Mary were not the only ones ruined by Mayerling. Whereas, in spite of his deep mourning, the Emperor sat at his desk on the day of his son's death dutifully to sign his papers, Elisabeth was restless. She could not grasp why her son had killed himself and had feelings of guilt because she had neglected him and took up the idea that she had to make contact with him. On February 9, 1889, the Empress went incognito in a fiacre to the Capuchin crypt, where she identified herself to the priest guardian and asked to be left alone with her son. Several times she called out aloud "Rudolf" and departed in bitter disappointment from the resting-place of the Habsburgs because he did not reply.

From that time on, Elisabeth wore mourning dress. Until her own frightful end—nine years after Mayerling, on the shores of Lake Geneva, at Geneva—she traveled incessantly.

After Rudolf's death and because of his wife's continual absence, the Emperor was more alone than ever. "Now I do not know how I shall endure life without my son who was my only joy and for whom I was working," he once said to Prince Heinrich Reuss, the German ambassador, who passed the words on to Emperor Wilhelm. "But I shall work for the monarchy and do my duty as long as my old bones hold on. God knows how long that will still be." It must be particularly painful for the Emperor, the Prince also reported to Berlin, that there was no letter for him found among the farewell letters.

Crown Prince Rudolf could no longer be mentioned in the presence of the Emperor; no public monuments were erected and his name was removed from all official papers. It could only continue to be said in the still incomplete edition of the *Kronprinzen Werk*, of which the last volume appeared in 1902, that it had begun at the suggestion of, and with contributions from, His Excellency Crown Prince Archduke Rudolf. Now his widow, Stéphanie, took over the sponsorship of the additional volumes.

In her memoirs, the Crown Princess describes how she reacted to her husband's death and his farewell letter: "Each word was like the blow of a dagger in my heart. A storm of indignation and revolt raged within me. What I had foreseen during the many solitary hours of silent, agonizing fear had become fact. My entire being rebelled against the disbelief, the wanton frivolity with which life had been thrown away."

After Rudolf's death, Stéphanie lived at first in complete isolation at the Viennese court. She took many trips, often accompanied by her daughter Elisabeth, and, eleven years after the tragedy at Mayerling she entered into a second marriage with the Hungarian Count Elemer Lónyay, which was not in accordance with her rank. She was separated from her daughter Elisabeth by the Emperor's command, inasmuch as the little archduchess could not live in the household of a count, following Habsburg tradition; for a long time she was not permitted to meet her mother's new husband and she was not allowed to attend their wedding. Count Lónyay was not elevated to the rank of prince (Fürst) until 1917, by Emperor Charles. Stéphanie lived together happily with her husband at his castle Oroszvar which the former Crown Princess had to abandon in flight in 1945 after the Russian invasion. She died shortly thereafter in the Benedectine abbey at Pannonhalma, where she had found refuge among members of that religious order.

Her daughter Elisabeth grew up under the guardianship of her grandfather Emperor Francis Joseph in the Laxenburg castle and at the Hofburg. Crown Prince Rudolf, at whose death she was five years old, remained her idol, whom she henceforth sought to emulate. As a little girl the archduchess was already known for her pronounced stubbornness. At 19 she contracted a morganatic marriage with Otto Windisch-Graetz, with whom she was not happy.

The conditions for happiness were anything but favorable. Elisabeth had lost her head over the handsome prince, but he was not prepared to break his engagement to another girl whom he really loved, as he informed the Emperor. Francis Joseph was not displeased at this, as he was hoping to find a husband of equal rank for his granddaughter belonging to a ruling house. However, when he disclosed to Elisabeth that Prince Windisch-Graetz was engaged to another girl, the archduchess burst into tears and seized the opportunity to say to the Emperor; "My father preferred to die rather than betray his love. I am like him. I too am not afraid of death, to which I shall give up my youth, because it alone can free one from suffering."

That was a threat to which Francis Joseph could see no alternative after all that had happened. He recalled the prince and told him that his granddaughter had such strong feelings that she would accept no refusal. Prince Otto again expressed his regret. He said that he had given his word to a young woman he loved and he could not break his word without forfeiting his honor as an aristocrat and officer.

There was a short pause after the prince had finished. Then Francis Joseph replied: "As your Emperor and Commander-in-Chief I command you to marry my granddaughter Archduchess Elisabeth Marie of Habsburg-Lorraine."

The cavalry officer had no choice but to click his heels and say "Yes, Your Majesty."

That sealed the next catastrophe in the House of Habsburg. Shortly before the wedding, the Emperor bestowed on Otto Windisch-Graetz the title of Fürst.[13] Elisabeth bore him four children. After three years of marriage, there came an explosion when she discovered her husband, whom she had placed under surveillance, *in flagrante delicto* in the arms of another woman. Elisabeth had hidden a pistol which she now aimed at her rival and fired. The prince's mistress, an opera singer named Marie Ziegler, was seriously wounded. For a year the Imperial censors were able to suppress this sensational story that the daughter of Crown Prince Rudolf had shot someone. In October, 1906, Marie Ziegler gave an interview

---

[13] After the 16th century, a title between duke and count.

to an American newspaper in which she described that act of jealousy on the part of the Emperor's granddaughter. Then the Austrian newspapers quoted from the article.

Seventeen years later, when her Imperial grandfather was dead and the monarchy dissolved, Elisabeth obtained a divorce.[14] Many years later, after the Second World War, she entered into a second marriage with Leopold Petznek, a Social Democratic teacher and politician, who had been her companion for many years. The "Red Archduchess," as she was often called, was herself a member of the Socialist Party and died in 1963 at the age of eighty.

The Vetsera and Baltazzi families became social exiles, because the Court passed on to them the principal guilt for the Crown Prince tragedy. Many of the once "good friends" of the jolly Baroness Helene Vetsera, who was so popular in Viennese society, did not even offer their condolences and when she purposely took a ride down the Prater Allee she often received no greeting. Thereupon she complained to Prime Minister Taaffe, who had to reply that he was unable to "influence the attitude of her acquaintances." Only, as a private person, as he expressly emphasized, he advised her "to spend some time abroad in order to avoid further affronts." And the Emperor, to whom she also wrote, had her advised by his Cabinet head "to bear the deep pain placed upon you by Providence with calm resignation and avoid everything which might hinder the gradual alleviation of the situation."

Helene Vetsera fled from Austria and hid for some time in Venice. She died on February 1, 1921, at the age of seventy-eight. She had survived all of her four children.

In her testament she asked her daughter-in-law, Margit

---

[14] The story of that marriage was recounted by Elisabeth's daughter-in-law, Ghislaine-Windisch-Graetz in her book *Kaiser Adler und Rote Nelke*.

Vetsera, to destroy all papers concerning Mayerling "in order that they may not fall into improper hands and be misused." Margit Vetsera carried out that last will and burned Mary's farewell letters, the original manuscript of Helene Vetsera's memoir, and her requests made to Francis Joseph. In addition, there was a letter from the coachman Bratfisch in which he informed Helene Vetsera that he was the last one who had spoken to her daughter and that she accepted her destiny with courage.

Even Countess Marie Larisch, who had once been the Empress' favorite niece, was treated like a leper after Mayerling. She could not be excused for having arranged the meetings between Mary and Rudolf and for having concealed and encouraged their liaison. No matter how much naïveté may be conceded in Mary's case, she still knew exactly what she would do to her friend through her spectacular death at Mayerling. There was also a farewell letter to Larisch: "Dear Marie! Forgive me all the pain that I have brought you. I thank you sincerely for everything you have done for me. If life should become hard for you after what we have done, and I am afraid that it will be, then follow us. It is the best you can do. Your Mary."

Completely impoverished, Larisch wrote in her memoirs in 1907 "the complete truth about Mayerling" and had a copy sent to the Emperor fresh from the press. Francis Joseph purchased the entire edition for 1.2 million crowns (corresponding to almost twice the cost of the Vienna Ferris wheel). Nevertheless, the countess published the book after his death. She died in 1940 in a home for the aged.

Today, Crown Prince Rudolf's former hunting lodge is a cloister for Carmelite nuns. Francis Joseph transferred it to that order, whose religious sisters have been praying daily for the Emperor, the Empress and their son. And for Mary Vetsera, "for all souls are alike in the Great Beyond." Here at least it is recognized that the little baroness was a creature of God, the same as the son of the Emperor.

Mayerling was completely rebuilt by the Carmelites, so that the cloister walls scarcely resemble those of the former hunting lodge. Where the Crown Prince's room was located, there is now a chapel; an altar stands on the site of the bed where Rudolf and Mary died.

Scarcely a year has passed since the frightful events at Mayerling without the appearance of new sensational stories. Self-styled "witnesses" constantly came to light who felt that they knew the truth and nothing but the truth. Aside from the contents of the mysterious casket which the Habsburg family is not prepared to make public, only one other document may exist which could stand up against a realistic reconstruction of the deed. It is the secret record of Count Taaffe, which is still now after more than a hundred years in the possession of relatives of the former Prime Minister. Shortly after the collapse of the monarchy, a member of the family was able to see those papers. That was Countess Zoe Wassilko-Serecki, and many years later, in September, 1955, she gave the contents in evidence to the Austrian government archives. Zoe Wasssilko was related both to Count Taaffe (one of the Emperor's few close friends) and also to the Chief of Police, Baron Krauss. Here is an excerpt from her statement:

"It was October, 1919. I was then a young girl at Ellischau Castle in Bohemia, the property of Count Taaffe. One evening Heinrich Taaffe, my cousin by marriage, the Prime Minister's son, asked me quite spontaneously whether I, as granddaughter of Baron Krauss, who was at that time Chief of Police, would be interested in reading the original papers on the Mayerling case which had been exchanged between his father and my grandfather . . . I took the records with me to my room and read them through with great interest and deepest compassion on that same night, some of them several times. The papers were all together in a longish envelope. It was a sheaf of twenty to thirty reports on heavy sheets of government paper. On the upper left was an official dry seal and above it the words 'Streng Reservat' (Note: Most Restricted). The address was: 'Prime Minister to the Chief of Police and vice versa.' Both were headed "Your Excellency."' The official correspondence contains the reports of the Court commission describing the situation during the hours and days after the catastrophe. According to the data, 'the Crown Prince was in a frightful condition, his brain sprayed forth and clinging partly to the walls. The revolver was found in or next to his hand. In the case of the baroness, her carotid artery had been hit from the side. A coagulated flow of blood extended from her open mouth to her feet.'"

The countess learned from the results of the post mortem examination "that Archduke Rudolf had shot himself in the mouth, which explained the shattering of the temple. Mary's corpse was examined at Mayerling. She was placed in a dark, dusty little storeroom and then laid naked onto a table; afterwards, completely covered with her clothes and her fur coat, she was simply left lying there."

Zoe Wassilko-Serecki declared in her official statement that these were the contents of the secret papers "from which I made a few notes. In any case, there was nothing there, not even the slightest suspicion, that the Crown Prince had been murdered and one cannot assume that those two highly-placed officials who had to work on this momentous case intended to conceal anything from each other. They concluded: With the girl's consent, the Crown Prince killed her and then himself."

The reason why none of the witnesses or politicians or officials involved with explaining it ever spoke about the circumstances surrounding Mayerling was a solemn oath each one had given the Emperor. Countess Wassilko-Serecki said that even her grandfather, Chief of Police Krauss, "never spoke with his family about the Crown Prince's death and no questions were to be asked him about it."

After the Second World War, part of the "Krauss papers" were discovered by accident in Berlin, where they had been brought by the Nazis. The "Taaffe papers" have remained lost up to now.

Even the prince's own coachman Bratfisch remained silent to the end of his life. He survived his master by less than four years, dying in December, 1892, at the age of only forty-five. His discretion was widely respected as being particularly noble. Nevertheless the man who knew everything about the Crown Prince's affairs and who had spent the last evening with Mary and Rudolf had been offered five million crowns to publish his memoirs. But he only said: "I am silent as a tomb. That is all I have to say." Of course, the Emperor must have sweetened his noble restraint with a monthly income for life.

After the grave robbery at Heiligenkreuz had been cleared up in December, 1992, the remains of Crown Prince Rudolf's mistress were taken into custody and locked up in a steel cabinet at the Institute for Forensic Medicine in Vienna. As soon as the current examinations are concluded, Mary Vetsera's mortal remains will again be buried in her grave, in order finally to come to rest. Hopefully, this time it will really be eternal.

Translator's Note

Mary Vetsera was reinterred in her original grave at Heiligenkreuz in October, 1993, in a brand-new coffin. In Vienna, the office of the Public Prosecutor declined to bring charges against Helmut Flatzelsteiner for the desecration of her grave. He still hopes to have the remains of Archduke Rudolf exhumed, but will probably find it more difficult to remove them "bei Nacht und Nebel" from the Capuchin crypt in Vienna.

APPENDIX

Crown Prince Rudolf As Lyricist
First Publication of His Viennese Songs

EIN EIGENER ZAUBER

Es liegt eine Gattin verzweifelt im Bett
Der Mann, der hat's g'heirat, aber mögen thut er's net,
Die Gschäften, die machen den Kopf ihm so schwer
Drum richt sie ein feines Souper immer her,
Trink, lieber Mann, stoß mit mir an,
Denn in ein so ein Glas Malaga Wein
Muß oft ein eigener Zauber sein.

An Alte voll Wimmerln mit der Nasen über's Eck
Hat a tamische Erbschaft g'macht, die Schachtel wird keck,
Sie hängt sich in einen Mann mit 25 Jahr
Und da wandeln die zwei am Galizinberg gar.
Ob denn dem jungen Herrn nicht übel wird werd'n!
Denn a so a alte Kraxen im Mondschein
Das muss ein eigener Zauber sein.
Das muss ein eigener Zauber sein.

Ein eigener Zauber.

1.

Es liegt eine Gattin verzweifelt im Bett
der Mann der hat g'heiret, aber mögen thut er's net,
die G'schäften die machen den Kopf ihm so schwer
drum ruft sie ein feiner Zauber immer her.
Trink lieber Mann, stoß mit mir an,
denn in ein so ein Glas Malaga Wein
Muß oft ein eigener Zauber sein.

2.

An alte voll Wimmerln mit der Nasen
                                   rikis Eck
Hat a Traunische Erbschaft g'macht, die
                              Schettel sind Reich,
Sie haugt sich ~~~~ in einen Mann mit
                                25 Jahr
Und da wandeln die zwei am Galizinberg,
                                      gar.
Ob denn den jungen Herrn rikis rikl
                         sind rendir,
Denn a so a alte Schraxen im Mondenschein
Das muß ein eigener Zauber sein.
Das muß ein eigener Zauber sein.

VERSCHIEDENE BEGRIFFE

Das die Geschäften schlecht gehen, sagt zu einer Gewissen,
Der Herr von Gehstoni, na, der wird's halt nicht wissen.
Die Sali, die Kecke, die sagt der dumme Kerl,
Der war halt noch niemals beim Sperl.
Oder am Kohlmarkt oder am Graben
Sonst müßt der an anderen Begriff davon haben.

Was Liebe ist, will die Nichte genau wissen
Das fahrt in Herrn Onkel in's Gwissen.
Und weil er herin nicht thun kann so wie er will,
So fahrt er's hinaus in die hintere Brühl.
Dort will ihr der Alte die Lieb expliciren
Na, die kann an sauberen Begriff davon krieg'n.

Es wart auf sei Liebste ein Liebster langmächtig,
Bei 30 Grad Kälten, es friert ihn schon prächtig.
Und macht dann die Liebste ein bitteres Gfries,
Weil halt der Liebste heut so ein Eiszapfen is'
Ja bleib du stehn bei derar Kälten zwei Stund auf der Stiegen
Da wirst schon an andern Begriff davon kriegen.

NA VERSTEHT SI!

Couplet

Bei an Fenster lahnt a Madel, auf der Gassen steht ein Herr,
Und da winkt sie mit an Tüchel ihn, also hergehst in ihr her,
Weil er gar nichts thut dergleichen, mach ich aufmerksam den
Mann
Doch der wird unbändi granti, und schreit mi ganz zornig an
Wegen der schwülen Luft nur geht sie, nur geht sie
Na versteht sie, na versteht sie, na versteht sie, wie's schon
is.
Na versteht sie, na versteht sie, na versteht sie, na ganz g'wiß

Eine Nähmamsell a schöne, die ich kenn schon lange Zeit
Arbeit gar nichts, aber tragt sich, wie die allerfeinsten Leut
Hat Braceletten, gold'ne Ringe, Ohrg'häng, Brosch und was
Gott was
Neuli frag ich ihr Frau Muata, sagen's woher hat die denn das
Sie sagt: Hemeda nur näht,—nur näht sie
Na versteht sie—etc. wie oben.

Eine andre will nix wissen, redt mit keinem Mann a Wort
Will so mancher sie zum Weibe, schickt sie alle zornig fort
Und will lieber ledig bleiben, heirath nur an reichen Mann
Wo sie's so recht nobel geben, eine Dame spielen kann
Einen Grafen halt gern hätt sie, gerne hatt sie, na versteht
sie—etc. etc.

A Familie gibt sehr nobel, möcht gern g'hören zur feinen Welt
Und hab'n oft daham nix z'essen, ewigs große Gfrett mit'n
Geld
Neuli geh i ins Versatzamt und siech ran a Dienerin
Mit an ungeheuren Binkel mitten unter d' andern drin
Aus Zerstreuung nur drin steht sie, drin steht sie
Naja versteht sie—etc. etc.

Eine Mutter sagt mein Töchterl, hörns mit der hab i a Freud

Die geht so viel gern in d' Kirchen, thut nur beten d'ganze Zeit
Gibt sich gar nicht ab mit d' Männer
Denn die san ihr viel zu keck
Kommt ihr aner nur in d' Nähe, schreit sie glei, fahrens ab,
 gehns weg
In der Kirchen kniat und beth sie, und beth sie,
Naja versteht si, ganz g'wiß beth sie, na versteht si—etc. etc.

EINST UND JETZT

Die Jungfrau mit goldigen Locken
Die Jungfrau mit goldigem Haar
Ein Schneider, der wollt sie verlocken
Sie führen zum Sperl sogar
Doch die Jungfrau mit goldigen Locken
Mit dem Herzen von Eisen und Stein
Die sagt gleich zum Schneider
Mondscheinsatz gehst weiter
Sonst laß i der die fünf Bahner spuren
Hau dich auf die Schneiderpapen
Daß die die Hobelscharten
Bis nach Mexiko fliegen.

Einst seufzte die Jungfrau hereuten
Wenn's in Jüngling von weiten that seh'n
Und der Jüngling seufzte dreuten
Da konnte doch sicher nichts gscheh'n
So seufzten sie Wochen und Jahre
Sie liebten sich bloß auf Distanz
A so a Gfrett giebts nimmer
Unsere Weana Kinder, Herrn und Damen schicken
  aufs Land hinaus
Voll Grasfleck, Gelsentipeln
Kommen dann die Sippeln
Ganz z'sammgearbeitet zu Haus.

Einst haben die Maiden die frommen
In ihrem schneeweißen zünftigen Kleid
Das Linnen am Spinnrad gesponnen
Das war noch für die Ritter a Zeit
Da hat's noch keine Maskenball 'geben
Da war noch ka Schmuck und ka Trigot
Beim Sperl zum umafetzen
Thuts a Bamwollfetzen, drum haben die Madeln
  jetzt ka Hemd an

Und dann erst zum Spinnen
Kann's kein Mensch mehr zwingen
Höchstens die Polizeidirection.

WIENER GFRETTG'SCHICHTEN
Couplet

A Schulbua, ganz a klaner,
Mit ana
Spatzenbauer auf der Gassen want ganz bitterlich,
Sagt s' is zum Teufel hol'n
Mir haben s' mei Madel g'stohl'n
Sie is mir untereu word'n
O fürchterlich,
Jetzt geht der Franz mit ihr
Und i, i hab' wegen ihr
Vom Lehr' Beutler kriegt
Vom Vater Schläg
Und jetzten auf der Schleifen
Z'bricht ma gar mei Pfeifen
Und mei Zigarispitz
Is des a Pech . . .

Wie so mancher Einer,
Geht ein Herr, ein feiner
Bimmelbamelbum in d' Stadt hinein
Mit'n Spezialzigarl
Sieht er no a Madl
Wigelwagelt er glei' hinterdrein.
Wie'r a Grenadiera
Kummt glei an'r füra
Schreit, g'selchter Mehlwurmbua,
Hörst, jetzt fahr a.
Aber liebes Fräulein bitt' Sie,
Bumms da liegt der Strizzi
Mit'n Spezialzigarl am Pflaster da!

Ein Herrn is z'Haus schon zwieder,
Wandelt treu und bieder
Weil grad Fruhjahr ist nach Grinzing naus.
Das Lüfterl denkt er sie,

150

A feine Landpartie
Die wird mir gut thun, geh 8 tag net z'Haus.
Hat auf a Bäuerin g'schaut,
Die Bauern habn 'n g'haut,
N' Tintsch antrieb'n und in a Lacken g'setzt.
Bei der Stallthür aussi g'flog'n
Hab'n ihm sein'n Frack auszog'n
Kummt ganz zermudelt an,
Der Biedermann.

Von süssem bangem Sehnen,
Unter Wehmuthsthränen
Seufzt ein Jüngling, drunt mit der Guitar.
Turteltaubengirren,
Amorflügelschwirren,
Dudelt, strudelt wir ein reiner Narr.
Er bimmelt, schwingelt, singelt,
Bis das Fenster klingelt
Kommt a Hand hervur
Mit 'ran Lawur.
Da wird ihm's Herz so schwer, 's Lavur is a schon leer,
Der Jüngling geht dahin
Und singt nicht mehr.

Es lobt ein Mann die Seine,
Sagt so wie die Meine,
Gibt's ka zweite mehr auf derer Welt.
Sie ist ein wahres Wunder,
Alles andere Plunder,
Gebet's schon net her um's theure Geld.
Da kummt sei Freund und sagt,
Wo hast denn dö z'sampackt
Das wahre Gimpelweibel, siechts und lacht,
Die is mit die tapfern Hess,
Im letzten Feldzug g'west,
Als Markadanterin, wünsch guate Nacht.

151

Bei der Gigaritschen, bei der Gagaratschen
Bei der goldan Latern
Mit der blitsowi Resi
Tanzt die Lusi d' Böse
Daß ma narrisch mocht' werd'n,
Thun an Cancan probir'n,
Die feschen Schritt riskir'n
So tanzens schiaberisch himmelhoch,
Die Zwoa,
Aber die Trikot san z'rissen,
Da haben's es aussi g'schmissen
D' Frala Lusi und di Resi a!

BIBLIOGRAPHY

BALTAZZI-SCHARSCHMID, Heinrich & SWISTUN, Hermann.
Die Familien Baltazzi-Vetsera im kaiserlichen Wien.
Vienna-Cologne-Graz: Styria, 1980.

BANKIER, Alexander A.
Ein Feind des Systems; Kronprinz Rudolf und die Freimaurerei, in: *Rudolf, ein Leben im Schatten von Mayerling.*
Vienna: Historisches Museum der Stadt Wien, 1990.

BANKL, Hans.
Woran sie wirklich starben. Krankheiten und Tod historischer Persönlichkeiten. Vienna-Munich-Bern: Wilhelm Maudrich, 1989.

BIBL, Viktor.
Thronfolger. Munich: Musarion, 1929.

BIBL, Viktor.
Kronprinz Rudolf. Leipzig: Gladius, 1939.

BROUCEK, Peter.
Kronprinz Rudolf und die Armee, in: *Rudolf, ein Leben im Schatten von Mayerling.* Vienna: Historisches Museum der Stadt Wien, 1990.

CORTI, Egon Caesar Conte.
Elisabeth, die seltsame Frau. Salzburg: Anton Pustet, 1934.

FEIGL, Erich.
Kaiserin Zita. Von Österreich nach Österreich. Vienna-Munich: Amalthea, 1982.

FLESCH-BRUNNINGEN, Hans.
Die letzten Habsburger in Augenzeugenberichten. Berlin-Darmstadt-Vienna: Karl Rauch, 1967.

FRANZEL, Emil.
Kronprinzen-Mythos und Mayerling-Legenden. Vienna-Munich: Herold, 1963.

FUGGER, Nora Fürstin.
Im Glanz der Kaiserzeit. Vienna: Amalthea, 1932.

GRÖSSING, Sigrid-Maria.

Amor im Hause Habsburg. Vienna: Kremayr & Scheriau, 1990.

GRUBER, Clemens M.
Die Schicksalstage von Mayerling. Nach Dokumenten und Aussagen. Judenburg: Erich Miakar, 1989.

HAMANN, Brigitte.
Rudolf, Kronprinz und Rebell. Vienna-Munich: Amalthea, 1978.

HAMANN, Brigitte.
Rudolf, Majestät, ich warne Sie . . . , Geheime und private Schriften. Vienna-Munich: Amalthea, 1979.

HOLLER, Gerd.
Mayerling, Neue Dokumente zur Tragödie, 100 Jahre danach. Vienna-Munich: Amalthea, 1988.

HUMMELBERGER, Walter.
Maria Caspar und Joseph Bratfisch, in: *Jahrbuch des Vereins für Geschichte der Stadt Wien*. Vienna, 1963/64.

JUDTMANN, Fritz.
Mayerling ohne Mythos. Vienna: Kremayr & Scheriau, 1968.

LERNET-HOLENIA, Alexander.
Mayerling. Hamburg, Vienna: Paul Zsolnay, 1960.

LOEHR, Clemens.
Mayerling. Vienna: Amalthea, 1968.

MARKUS, Georg.
Der Kaiser Franz Joseph I. in Bildern und Dokumenten. Vienna-Munich: Amalthea, 1985.

MARKUS, Georg.
Geschichten der Geschichte. Vienna-Munich: Amalthea, 1991.

MARKUS, Georg.
G'schichten aus Österreich. Zwischen gestern und heute. Vienna-Munich: Amalthea, 1987.

MARKUS, Georg.
Katharina Schratt. Die heimliche Frau des Kaisers. Vienna-Munich: Amalthea, 1982.

MATTL-WURM, Sylvia.
Es hat noch keine Frau gegeben, die mir widerstanden hatte. Der Kronprinz und die Frauen, in: *Rudolf, ein Leben im Schatten von Mayerling*. Vienna: Historisches Museum der Stadt Wien, 1990.
Das Mayerling-Original.
Offizieller Akt des k.k. Polizeipräsidiums. Munich-Stuttgart-Vienna-Zurich: Wilhelm Frick, 1955.
MITIS, Oskar Freiherr von.
Das Leben des Kronprinzen Rudolf. Vienna: Herold, 1928.
RADZIWILL, Princess Catherine.
Meine Erinnerungen. Leipzig: Glaudius, 1905.
SALVENDY, John T.
Rudolf, Psychogramm eines Kronprinzen. Vienna-Munich: Amalthea, 1987.
SOKOP, Brigitte.
Jene Gräfin Larisch. Vienna-Cologne-Graz: Böhlau, 1985.
STÉPHANIE, Princess of Belgium.
Ich sollte Kaiserin werden. Leipzig: Glaudius, 1935.
SWISTUN, Hermann.
Mary Vetsera, Gefährtin für den Tod. Vienna-Cologne-Graz: Styria, 1983.
TÖTSCHINGER, Gerhard.
Auf den Spuren der Habsburger. Vienna-Munich: Amalthea, 1992.
TOMICZEK, Herbert.
Kronprinz Rudolf als Jäger, in: *Rudolf, ein Leben im Schatten von Mayerling*. Vienna: Historisches Museum der Stadt Wien, 1990.
WALCHER, Maria.
Das Wienerlied zur Zeit des Thronfolgers, in: *Rudolf, ein Leben im Schatten von Mayerling*. Vienna: Historisches Museum der Stadt Wien, 1990.
WALTHER, Susanne.
Aus den späteren Lebensjahren des Thronfolgers, in: *Rudolf. Ein Leben im Schatten von Mayerling*. Vienna: Historisches

Museum der Stadt Wien, 1990.

WEISSENSTEINER, Friedrich.
Lieber Rudolf. Briefe von Kaiser Franz Joseph und Elisabeth an ihren Sohn. Vienna: Ueberreuter, 1991.

WEISSENSTEINER, Friedrich.
Reformer, Republikaner und Rebellen. Das andere Haus Habsburg-Lothringen. Vienna: Österreichischer Bundesverlag, 1987.

WINDISCH-GRAETZ, Ghislaine.
Kaiseradler und rote Nelke. Das Leben der Tochter des Kronprinzen Rudolf. Vienna-Munich: Amalthea, 1988.

INDEX OF NAMES

D

DÄNZER, Georg 94
DARWIN, Charles 46
DESMINES, Thomas 17
DICHAND, Hans 13, 14,
16, 18, 20, 32, 33, 36,
42
DRAGON, Friedrich 16,
33
DUBRAY, Gabriel 24

E

EDELBACHER, Max 33,
34
EDWARD VII, King of
England 25, 49
EICHENSEDER, Herbert
33
ELISABETH, Archduchess
84, 87, 88, 109, 111,
134
ELISABETH, Empress 23,
44, 45, 52, 70, 82, 83,
94, 126, 133

F

FEIGL, Erich 64
FELLINGER, Karl 3
FERENCZY, Ida von 122,
126
FESTETICS, Marie
Countess 83
FISCHER, Josef 11, 75
FLATZELSTEINER, Hel-

mut 2, 3, 10, 12, 13,
14, 15, 16, 17, 19, 20,
33, 34, 35, 38, 39, 40,
41, 42, 43, 55, 56, 57,
59, 67, 72, 73, 74,
104, 105, 106
FRANZ FERDINAND,
Archduke 49, 54, 71,
78, 96, 101, 109
FRANCIS JOSEPH I,
Emperor of Austria 23,
44. 45, 46, 47, 50, 51,
54, 63, 64, 70, 71, 78,
79, 90, 100, 113, 126,
127
FRANZEL, Emil 69, 70
FRANZ SALVATOR,
Archduke 121
FREUD, Sigmund 34
FREY, Nora 65
FRIEDRICH III, German
Emperor 25, 49
FRIEDRICH, Archduke
109
FUGGER, Nora, Fürstin 24
FUTTERKNECHT, Chris-
tian 104

G

GALIMBERTI, Luigi 70
GIESL-GIESLINGEN,
Arthur, Freiherr von
117, 129
GINDELY, Anton 53
GISELA, Archduchess 63
GONDRECOURT, Leo-

The well-known Viennese author and journalist, Georg Markus, describes two sensational crimes in his latest book *Crime at Mayerling: The Life and Death of Mary Vetsera*. He has documented in an exciting and informative manner the background of the tragedy that involved the Crown Prince of Austria and his eighteen-year-old mistress and the spectacular theft of Baroness Vetsera's remains from her grave. These thrilling events are confirmed by numerous photographs and research material.

Bild, Munich

Georg Markus describes two crimes that have attracted the greatest attention of all time: in January, 1889, the corpses of Crown Prince Rudolf and of his mistress were found at Mayerling castle near Vienna. And in December, 1992, came the news of the theft of the remains of Baroness Mary Vetsera. The background of both crimes is documented in this fascinating book.

Appenzeller Zeitung

Journalist Solves a Century-Old Puzzle.
The man who brought an end to a century of speculation: Georg Markus, a Viennese newspaperman, has discovered what has troubled Austrians since 1889. His research has revealed how Baroness Mary Vetsera, the mistress of Crown Prince Rudolf, really died in January, 1889.

Münchener Merkur

After the spectacular desecration of the grave, the events at Mayerling appear in a new light. For the first time, the tragedy can be understood through the expert opinions of the forensic medical specialists.

Kleine Klosterneuburger Zeitung